Yankees in Michigan

DISCOVERING THE PEOPLES OF MICHIGAN

Arthur W. Helweg, Russell M. Magnaghi, and Linwood H. Cousins, Series Editors

Ethnicity in Michigan: Issues and People
Jack Glazier and Arthur W. Helweg

French Canadians in Michigan John P. DuLong	*Hungarians in Michigan* Éva V. Huseby-Darvas
African Americans in Michigan Lewis Walker, Benjamin C. Wilson, and Linwood H. Cousins	*Mexicans and Mexican Americans in Michigan* Rudolph Valier Alvarado and Sonya Yvette Alvarado
Albanians in Michigan Frances Trix	*Scots in Michigan* Alan T. Forrester
Jews in Michigan Judith Levin Cantor	*Greeks in Michigan* Stavros K. Frangos
Amish in Michigan Gertrude Enders Huntington	*Chaldeans in Michigan* Mary C. Sengstock
Italians in Michigan Russell M. Magnaghi	*Latvians in Michigan* Silvija D. Meija
Germans in Michigan Jeremy W. Kilar	*Arab Americans in Michigan* Rosina J. Hassoun
Poles in Michigan Dennis Badaczewski	*Irish in Michigan* Seamus P. Metress and Eileen K. Metress
Dutch in Michigan Larry ten Harmsel	*Scandinavians in Michigan* Jeffrey W. Hancks
Asian Indians in Michigan Arthur W. Helweg	*Cornish in Michigan* Russell M. Magnaghi
Latinos in Michigan David A. Badillo	*Belgians in Michigan* Bernard A. Cook
South Slavs in Michigan Daniel Cetinich	*Copts in Michigan* Eliot Dickinson

Discovering the Peoples of Michigan is a series of publications examining the state's rich multicultural heritage. The series makes available an interesting, affordable, and varied collection of books that enables students and lay readers to explore Michigan's ethnic dynamics. A knowledge of the state's rapidly changing multicultural history has far-reaching implications for human relations, education, public policy, and planning. We believe that Discovering the Peoples of Michigan will enhance understanding of the unique contributions that diverse and often unrecognized communities have made to Michigan's history and culture.

Yankees in Michigan

Brian C. Wilson

Michigan State University Press

East Lansing

♾ The paper used in this publication meets the minimum requirements
of ANSI/NISO Z39.48-1992 (R 1997) (Permanence of Paper).

Michigan State University Press
East Lansing, Michigan 48823-5245

Printed and bound in the United States of America.

14 13 12 11 10 09 08   1 2 3 4 5 6 7 8 9 10

ISBN: 978-0-87013-825-6

LIBRARY OF CONGRESS CATALOGING-IN-PUBLICATION DATA

Wilson, Brian C.
Yankees in Michigan / Brian C. Wilson.
p. cm. — (Discovering the peoples of Michigan) '
Includes bibliographical references and index.
ISBN 978-0-87013-825-6 (pbk. : alk. paper)
1. New Englanders—Michigan—History. 2. Pioneers—Michigan—History.
3. Internal migrants—Michigan—History. 4. Michigan—History. 5. Frontier and pioneer life—
Michigan. 6. Michigan—Social life and customs. 7. Michigan—Social conditions.
8. Regionalism—Michigan—History. 9. Regionalism—Middle West—History. I. Title.
F575.A1W55 2008
304.8'77407409034—dc22
2008015190

Cover design by Ariana Grabec-Dingman
Book design by Sharp Des!gns, Lansing, Michigan
Cover photo is courtesy of Western Michigan University Archives and Regional History Collections.

Michigan State University Press is a member of the Green Press Initiative and is committed
to developing and encouraging ecologically responsible publishing practices. For more information about the Green Press Initiative and the use of recycled paper in book publishing,
please visit *www.greenpressinitiative.org*.

Visit Michigan State University Press on the World Wide Web at *www.msupress.msu.edu*

ACKNOWLEDGMENTS

Many people helped me in the research and writing of this book. For their patience and advice, I would especially like to thank series editors Art Helweg (Western Michigan University) and Russell Magnaghi (Northern Michigan University), and Julie L. Loehr, Assistant Director/Editor in Chief at the Michigan State University Press. Professor Gregory S. Rose (Department of Geography, The Ohio State University) graciously took the time to give the manuscript a thorough critical reading; his invaluable suggestions and corrections helped greatly to improve the finished book (all remaining errors, of course, are mine alone). Also, special thanks to Jim Zemke of Vermontville, Michigan, who one fine spring day dropped everything to give my wife and me an impromptu tour of the wonderful Vermontville Historical Museum; and special thanks to Sharon Carlson, Director and University Archivist, Western Michigan University Archives and Regional History Collections, Kalamazoo, Michigan, who did yeoman's service researching the pictures for this volume. Finally, I would like to dedicate *Yankees in Michigan* to my wife, Cybelle Shattuck, and to my good friend Richard Merkel.

Contents

APPENDICES

Introduction

Come all ye Yankee Farmers,

Who'd like to change your lot,

Who've spunk enough to travel

Beyond your native spot,

And leave behind the village

Where Pa' and Ma' do stay,

Come follow me and settle

In *Michigania.*

—From "Emigrant's Song," first published in a Detroit newspaper in 1831

In the summer of 1822, a stout young man with a broad forehead, deep-set eyes, and a determined expression stepped ashore and wandered into the raw streets of frontier Detroit. His name was Lucius Lyon, and if ever there was a man who epitomized the "spunky" Yankee, it was he.[1] Born at the turn of the nineteenth century in Shelburne, Vermont, Lyon came from a middling background and had only a common school education and four years' experience as an apprentice surveyor. At twenty-two, he had no money and scant prospects in his native New England. Faced with this, Lyon did what many young Yankees of his time and situation were doing: he headed west to the Michigan Territory to make his fortune. After toiling there nearly a decade as deputy surveyor general, during which time he tramped countless miles through the wilderness of what is now southern Michigan, northern Illinois, and southern Wisconsin, Lyon—much to his own surprise—found himself elected a territorial delegate to the U.S. Congress in 1833. He acquitted himself well in Washington. He defended Michigan's right to speedy state-hood and promoted internal improvements such as lighthouses and harbors. Eventually, Lyon would go on to participate in the drafting of Michigan's first constitution, and he served as one of Michigan's first senators after statehood in 1837, and again as a member of the House of Representatives in 1843. Along the way, the indefatigable Lyon found time to serve on the Board of Regents of the fledgling University of Michigan; help plat Grand Rapids and the village of Lyons in Ionia County; pioneer the commercial exploitation of brine pools for salt; bankroll Hiram Moore's invention of a mechanical "combine" harvester; and, finally, promote the Swedenborgian faith and champion temperance reforms. Although penniless and friendless when he arrived, Lyon's drive, business shrewdness, and civic-mindedness served him well as he carved out a notable place for himself in his adopted state.

While hardly typical in his talents and success, Lucius Lyon nevertheless typified many of the distinctive, if sometimes contradictory, traits that New Englanders brought with them to Michigan. Acquisitive yet philanthropic, independent yet voluntaristic, pious and moralistic yet pragmatic, Yankees vigorously sought to impose their particular ideas of proper behavior and social order wherever they went. Taken collectively, their influence on Michigan was formidable. During the period when Michigan transitioned from territory to state, Yankees, either directly from New England or after a generation in Upstate New York ("Yankee-Yorkers"), immigrated here in such abundance that, for a time, they represented the state's largest ethnic group. The 1850 Federal Census of the United States places the combined numbers of Yankees and Yankee-Yorkers in Michigan at 164,679, roughly 41.3 percent of the state's total population. By 1860 this proportion had fallen to 34 percent, yet Yankees still comprised 51 percent of all farmers and 48 percent of all heads of households.[2] From the beginnings of statehood, then, Yankees were in a position to stamp Michigan in their own image; given their energy and activism, not to mention their self-righteousness and sense of cultural superiority, they proceeded to do just that.

Lucius Lyon. (Courtesy of Burton Historical Collections, Detroit Public Library.)

Yankees like Lucius Lyon influenced all aspects of the political, social, and cultural life of early Michigan. In the antebellum period, Yankees surveyed, bought, and sold land purchased from the government, created prosperous farms, and built villages and towns, schools and churches, libraries and courthouses. Many Yankees worked hard to integrate the Michigan agricultural market into the national market economy, and just as many brought to Michigan a zeal for education, religion, and social reform. Yankees were in the forefront of abolitionism and were instrumental in the creation of the Republican Party. After the Civil War, Yankees and their progeny aggressively developed Michigan's industries, with New England capital crucial in financing large-scale mining, logging, railroad, and manufacturing operations. Not all the Yankee legacy is positive, as we shall see; however, it is safe to say that Michigan today would be a radically different place without its Yankee past.

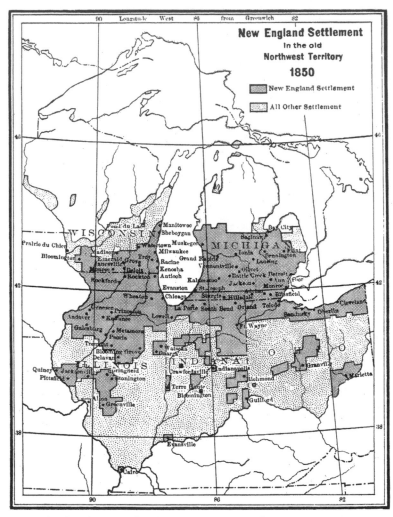

New England Settlement in the Old Northwest Territory. (From Lois Kimball Mathews,
The Expansion of New England [1909; reprin., New York: Russell & Russell, Inc., 1962].)

Yankee Impact on the Midwest and the Nation

Michigan during the nineteenth century had one of the highest concentrations of Yankees outside the Northeast, but the presence of Yankees was
hardly unique to the state. During the early national period, thousands of
Yankees streamed out of New England into Upstate New York and then into

the Western Reserve of Ohio, northern Illinois, southern Michigan, southeastern Wisconsin, southern Minnesota, the center of the Dakotas, Iowa, and parts of Kansas.[3] Eventually, Yankees would reach Oregon, Washington, California, and Hawaii. Later historians and geographers would call this vast region of Yankee settlement variously "the Yankee West," "Greater New England," "New England Extended," "New England Expanded," "Yankeedom," or "Yankeeland."[4] They would also point to the cohesiveness of Yankee culture in the Old Northwest as one of the decisive factors in the making of the modern Midwest. This is not to deny, of course, the contributions of other ethnic groups to the region. As the geographer D. W. Meinig reminds us, "In all but one [Michigan] of these western states Yankees were in the minority, in many cases a vociferous and influential minority, but nevertheless forced by the capacious boundaries of these new geopolitical units to compete for political power with large bodies of people who had very different outlooks and agendas."[5] Yankees, however, were uniquely suited to the rough and tumble of political and cultural competition on the American frontier. To a remarkable degree, they managed to impose many of their attitudes, values, and institutions on the inchoate societies of the Midwest, and long after the Yankee ethnic label had fallen into disuse in the region, the descendents of the original Yankee settlers would continue to consider themselves quintessential Midwesterners.[6] Despite the hubris of this claim, Yankees undeniably did have a substantial impact on the formation of the American heartland. To understand the history of Yankees in Michigan, therefore, is to begin to understand an important aspect of the larger story of the creation of Midwestern identity.

Yankees in New England and Beyond

New England "Yankees" comprised a true ethnic group in Colonial America. Not only was their culture distinctive, but they themselves were acutely conscious of it. When they began to move westward in the 19th century, they were intent on making their values the values of the entire nation.

—John G. Rice, "The Old-Stock Americans," 1981

Today when we think of the word "Yankee," we often think of it simply as a synonym for "American," or, more specifically, as the nickname for Union Army soldiers during the Civil War, or perhaps even a baseball team based in New York. During the eighteenth and nineteenth centuries, however, "Yankee" designated a distinct ethnic group, if by that term we mean a group "with a shared culture and sense of identity based on religion, race, and nationality."[7] Yankees were fiercely proud to be the descendents of the first seventeenth-century English settlers to New England; in fact, the word Yankee most plausibly can be traced to the guttural Indian pronunciation of "English" or "*Anglais.*"[8] Yankees traced their religious roots to the Puritan Calvinism that dominated colonial New England. While Yankee religion would in time be fragmented into a dozen different denominations, most retained the uncompromising seriousness, distrust of innate human goodness,

7

and concern for the social order that marked the old Puritan tradition. Race and religion, as for most ethnic groups, went hand in hand for these people. Well into the nineteenth century, Yankees would continue to celebrate the purity of what one Detroit minister would call their "Puritanized Anglo Saxon Blood." As for nationality, this too was clear: long after the United States had been established, Yankees maintained a strong sense that New England, not the United States, was "their nation."[9] Indeed, the first secessionist movement in this country did not arise in the south, but in New England in 1814, when, in protest of the War of 1812, delegates to the Hartford Convention proposed that the New England states secede from the Union and form a separate nation.

That Yankees were a separate people, Yankees themselves had no doubt. In other regions of the country, too, Yankee ethnicity was widely recognized, if hardly celebrated. Throughout the nineteenth century, Yankees were routinely portrayed humorously as stock characters in newspaper articles, novels, and plays written outside of New England. Ichabod Crane, Washington Irving's hapless schoolmaster in "The Legend of Sleepy Hollow," was, from his faintly ridiculous biblical name all the way to his choice of profession, the very embodiment of the stereotypical Yankee. The novelist James Fenimore Cooper, of Pennsylvania Quaker antecedents, had an especially virulent dislike of Yankees, notorious as they were for "pedantry, bad manners, slyness, cant, and self-satisfaction," not to mention bad cooking and a deplorable nasal twang. "Nothing Yankee agrees with me," Cooper once wrote, and it is not surprising that most of the villains in his novels hail from New England.[10]

Perhaps the best indication of the status of Yankees as a widely recognized ethnic group was the fact that the other major "homegrown" ethnic group in the United States—white Southerners—pursued an intense political and cultural rivalry with New Englanders, a rivalry that would ultimately define the nation. According to historian Robert Kelly, "Until they settled their account, American politics was essentially bipolar. The South and Yankeedom (the world of New England at home or transplanted), two expansive and self-conscious cultures struggling for national supremacy, created the nation's central cultural political conflict and the great crisis that culminated in the Civil War."[11] The fact that Yankees won that contest perhaps explains why today "Yankee" has become generalized to all Americans and lost its ethnic ring. Back in the day, however, while the issue was still in doubt, "Yankee" stood for a people apart who cherished a specific regional history and a set of values and aspirations deeply rooted in that history.

Yankee Origins

Yankees trace their origins to the successive waves of English migration to the rocky shores around Cape Cod, beginning with the landing of the *Mayflower* in 1620 and reaching its peak with the *Arbella* flotilla in 1630.[12] By 1640, some twenty-one thousand people had made the Atlantic passage and established themselves along the coastline of what had lately come to be marked on maps as New England. The majority of these colonists came from East Anglia, especially the counties of Suffolk, Essex, and Cambridge, while a substantial minority was drawn from the West Country counties of Dorset, Somerset, and Wiltshire. Eventually, a representative of every English country could be found in the New England colonies, although the East Anglians, from whom the distinctive Yankee nasal twang would later develop, dominated the colonies' principal settlement, Boston.[13]

In many ways, the colonization of New England was unique. While most of England's overseas possessions were colonies of exploitation, and therefore primarily attractive to unattached males, the New England colonies from the beginning were envisaged as colonies of settlement and attracted family groups—94 percent of all migrants were so attached, the greatest immigration of entire families in American history. Also unique was the colonists' social station. According to historian David H. Fischer, "The great majority [of heads of households] were yeoman, husbandmen, artisans, craftsmen, merchants and traders—the sturdy middle class of England." Thus, they "tended to be exceptionally literate, highly skilled, and heavily urban in their English origins."[14] While many immigrants to other English colonies sought to make their fortunes and return as quickly as they came, immigrants to New England brought their fortunes with them and sought to reproduce in America the urbane and largely urban middle-class lifestyles they had enjoyed in England.

There was another aspect that distinguished this English migration to America: it was conceived and controlled by Puritans. Puritans were strict Calvinists who sought to purify the Anglican Church of all its "Catholic" elements. They further sought to create a perfect Calvinist commonwealth in England in imitation of Jean Calvin's Geneva. When these goals met with resistance and persecution, Puritan leaders such as John Winthrop looked to America to find the freedom to build their "City upon a Hill." Not all migrants to New England were Puritans, but the majority was, including the leading families who would form a durable Puritan oligarchy that persisted well into the seventeenth century. It was they who directed the creation and maintenance of what they called Bible commonwealths, theocracies in which church and state worked hand in hand to preserve God's covenants with a fallen humanity. In addition to the earlier Plymouth Plantation of separatist Pilgrims (1620) and Winthrop's Puritan Massachusetts Bay Colony, two more such Bible commonwealths would be founded in colonial New England: Connecticut (1636) and New Haven (1637).

The idea of covenant was key to Puritan theology. A covenant is literally a contract or agreement between God and his people. The original covenant, called by Puritans the "Covenant of Works," was made with Adam, whom God guaranteed eternal life if he respected certain limits on his actions. When Adam transgressed these limits, God declared the contract invalid, damning the vast majority of Adam's descendents to Hell and everlasting punishment. God was not entirely vindictive, though. In his mercy he made another covenant, the "Covenant of Grace." By this covenant, God promised that despite the utter depravity of their fallen nature, a few people would be saved. Puritans believed also that God had already decided who would be saved before the beginning of time, thus predestining an elect few to salvation and the rest of humanity to eternal perdition. Nothing one did in this life could affect one's status, but at least God did guarantee that some unworthy few would enjoy heaven.[15]

Predestination, as historian David Fischer put it, may have been "one of the most harsh and painful creeds that believing Christians have ever inflicted upon themselves," but Puritans sincerely held and fervently believed in the doctrine.[16] This had manifold psychological and social consequences. Although Calvin himself said that God's will was inscrutable in this matter, and thus whether one was among the elect could never be known, Puritans nevertheless looked obsessively for signs of their election. They searched their consciences and their actions for evidence of their faith, a process that could lead alternately to moods of elation and despair. Puritans often recorded their introspection in detailed letters and diaries, which, even today, demonstrate an extraordinary level of psychological subtlety and discernment. It was natural that such acute self-consciousness and self-scrutiny would lead to high levels of discipline in both thought and behavior.

Where Puritan discipline manifested itself most conspicuously was in their day-to-day interactions with the larger world. Puritans believed with Martin Luther that Christians were obligated not only to live a godly interior life, but also to treat their life's work—their calling or "vocation"—as another means to worship God and do God's work in the world. Puritans, whether farmers, merchants, fishermen, or day laborers, all brought to the mundane tasks of their occupations the same kind of discipline they exercised in their interior life. Discipline meant not only a systematic approach to the tasks at hand, but also an intense energy that abhorred idleness. Time was sacred and must always be well used; ill use would provoke God's wrath. Constant productive activity, known as "improving the time," came to be a compulsion among Puritans, and time wasting, where it was not actually illegal (as it was in Massachusetts), would at least engender intense feelings of guilt. Efficiency became a watchword and valued in every aspect of life. Puritan diaries are filled with expressions of regret over misspent time, and one wag later quipped that Puritans "invented the rocking chair so that they could keep moving even while sitting still."[17] At a very early date, personal discipline and an industriousness bordering on compulsiveness became hallmarks of the people of New England.[18]

Puritan vocational discipline and industriousness resulted, more often than not, in business success. In some cases, it led to substantial wealth. And yet, success and wealth were never interpreted as goals in and of themselves. Puritans often saw both as sources of temptation that must be carefully managed. Conspicuous consumption was frowned upon, and excess in any area of life was a mark of ungodliness. Moreover, social rank was still ascribed by birth and lineage in Puritan New England; for someone to try to use their wealth to rise above their station was a sin and a threat to the stability of the community—obviously not the actions of the elect. The best thing one could do, then, was to reinvest profits back into one's business, which in turn inevitably improved profits. As a result, two more cultural traits that came to define New Englanders were an inveterate parsimony and a willingness to delay gratification to achieve larger ends.

As the sociologist Max Weber once observed, the Puritans' "Protestant ethic" embodied attitudes that were perfectly suited to the rise of industrial capitalism.[19] That industrial capitalism would not develop in New England until the eighteenth century, however, was due in part to the fact that another crucial element for this kind of economic system—individualism—was not valued by Puritans. Indeed, Puritan New England was a strongly communal society that stressed conformity and socioeconomic conservatism. Again, Puritans anchored their communalism in the notion of covenant. Just as God had made the Covenant of Grace with all of humanity, God also made covenants with specific peoples, as witnessed by his covenant with the Israelites of the Old Testament. New England Puritans believed they were heirs to this covenant, and because of this, they formed a "saved and saving remnant" called out from the world to create a godly society as a model to the rest of the world. That they were indeed God's "chosen people" would be proven in large part by the kind of society they created in America: if righteous, then God would help their enterprise prosper; if not, God would bring disaster. The health of the social order, therefore, was of intense concern to Puritans. Every aspect of public morality, civic life, and the economy was supervised, and infractions corrected with rigor. Laxness was an invitation to God's wrath, not to mention an indication that New England's Puritans were in danger of losing the covenant just as the Ancient Israelites had. Thus in the notion of covenant were born three more defining traits of New Englanders: a sense of chosenness as a people, a concomitant anxiety that they could lose this special status if they displeased God, and an abiding concern with the righteousness and stability of the social order.

To safeguard the social order, the Puritans depended on a triumvirate of formal institutions. The church, of course, was central, but civil government as exercised through the New England town was vital as well. However, what tied these two together and allowed them to function was the school. From the beginning of Puritan settlement in New England, education was a central concern. Laws in all the Puritan colonies obligated parents to teach their children how to read and write. As early as 1647, Massachusetts passed a statute requiring every town with fifty families to hire a schoolmaster, and those with a hundred families to offer Greek and Latin in their schools. The purpose of these schools—for every child to gain firsthand knowledge of the Bible—was made clear in the preamble to the statute: "It being one chief project of that old deluder, Satan, to keep men from the knowledge of the scriptures, as in former times keeping them in an unknown tongue, . . . that so at least the true sense and meaning of the Original might be clouded with false glosses of saint-seeming deceivers," literacy would be enjoined by law.[20] The "Old Deluder Law," as it came to be known, was important not only for the preservation of the church, but, as Puritan laws were presumed to be biblically based, was also essential for successful civil government. Finally, while a grammar school was adequate for the needs of a town, it was not sufficient for the needs of a colony. An elite class of men needed to be trained as ministers and magistrates to administer the Bible commonwealths at the highest levels. For this reason, Puritans early on supported higher education, founding four colleges before the Revolutionary War. For Puritans, education at all levels would always remain a priority, as it would for generations of their descendents.

From Puritan to Yankee

From the 1660s on, major changes began to occur in New England. In 1662, many Puritan congregations adopted the so-called Half-Way Covenant, which liberalized access to church membership and, in the case of Massachusetts and New Haven, gave greater access to full citizenship. Then, in 1690, representatives of the English King wrested political power from the oligarchs, disrupting the Puritans' theocratic government and imposing a limited religious freedom for non-Puritans. Anglicans, Baptists, and Quakers all began to compete for members with the old Puritan churches, now called Congregational churches. Furthermore, increased royal control bound the New England colonies closer to the Mother Country, exposing New Englanders to cultural, political, and economic forces that would fundamentally change their society. Enlightenment rationalism challenged elements of Puritan theology, radical republican ideas began to filter across the Atlantic, and the influence of a global market economy came to be strongly felt. Boston and the other seaport towns became more cosmopolitan, while the interior towns became wealthier and more refined. In short, New England became more modern and, subsequently, more secular and individualistic.

The cumulative effect of modernization on the people of New England was a gradual transition from "Puritan" to "Yankee."[21] While fundamental character traits such as discipline, industry, delayed gratification, and a reverence for education were now a part of the "cultural genes," Yankees differed in profound ways from their Puritan forebears.[22] For one thing, Yankees manifested a greater sense of independence and willingness to question established authority. Where once Puritans deferred to their ecclesiastical and governmental betters, Yankees became more assertive and insistent on the individual's right to think for him- or herself. In part this was due to the rise of denominational pluralism in New England: the novel possibility of religious choice in the colony led ineluctably to a need to justify one's rejection of the old Puritan faith. New political ideas emanating from England and Europe also played a major role in this shift. Republican ideals may have come late to the Puritan colonies, but they sank such deep roots there that New England would soon develop into a hotbed of political rebellion and become the first battlefield of the Revolutionary War. A testy independence bordering on crankiness became a defining Yankee characteristic.

Just as strikingly, Yankees came to see wealth and economic success as valuable in and of themselves—an attitude that would have appalled their pious ancestors.[23] Puritans had regarded unbridled material acquisitiveness as sinful, and for this reason, Puritan magistrates had maintained tight control over the colonial economy. Beginning late in the seventeenth century, however, the developing capitalist economies of England and Europe made deep inroads into New England. This forced a sweeping liberalization of colonial markets, which in turn led to the forging of new attitudes and behaviors. As a result, in the decades leading up to Independence, outside observers started to note a growing avarice among New Englanders that led to hard bargaining and sharp dealing. It appears that once the social and religious controls over the economy had been removed, the Puritans' "Protestant ethic" quickly morphed into the Yankee "spirit of capitalism," a frank and calculating cupidity that valued profit-getting above most else. This had profound social consequences for New England: where birth once determined social rank, now wealth and the ability to get wealth played a larger role. Great social mobility was still unusual during this period, but Yankees of middling origins could now at least aspire to a place in gentry and greater social power. With such a prize in sight, it was no wonder that competition in business became fierce and occasionally unprincipled, and that Yankees came to be stereotyped in other regions of the country as shrewd and greedy.

In one crucial respect, the modernization of New England led to an intensification, not a decline, of religious motivation among Yankees. They continued to believe strongly that they were God's chosen people and that the health of their society was a sign of God's covenant with them. Alarmingly, though, the rapid social changes of the period—precisely those changes that fostered Yankee independence and avarice—were also seen as threats to the social order. For many, this presaged the loss of New England's chosen status, not to mention an invitation to God's wrath. The churches in response stepped up efforts to curb the increasing social chaos of the age. Congregationalist ministers, for example, frequently addressed social concerns from their pulpits in Jeremiads, a sermonic form taking as its inspiration the Old Testament prophet Jeremiah's criticisms of a corrupt Israel. Moreover, a large-scale religious revival took place in New England during the 1730s and 1740s. Called the First Great Awakening, this series of revivals has long been interpreted by scholars as a collective attempt to turn back the clock and return New England to the more God-focused society of the original Puritan settlers.[24] While impossible, of course, the Awakening did lead to the rise of an aggressive moralism among Yankees. Puritans had always been keen to monitor their neighbors' behavior in a communal effort to preserve the social order, and Yankees continued the practice with a vengeance. As one contemporary observer put it, Yankees were famous for "the holy enterprise of minding other people's business."[25] Non-Yankees were often taken aback by the willingness of Yankees to publicly criticize their neighbors' behavior and bully them into conforming to community norms. Yankees, however, did not see this as gratuitous in the least: nothing less than the cosmic fate of an entire people depended on it. This sense of fragile covenantal chosenness—and the social concern and intense moralism it provoked—formed a fundamental and durable facet of the Yankee psyche.

The Yankee Diaspora

Given the relatively healthy climate, and taking seriously the biblical injunction to be fruitful and multiply, the population of New England grew at a rapid rate. Yankees doubled their numbers every generation for two centuries.[26] The first Puritan generations were confined largely to the coastal areas due to tight theocratic control over town founding, and to the threat of Indian attack.

Once control over town founding loosened and the Indian threat reduced, especially after the French and Indian War (1755–63), Yankees, typically as family groups, began to spread into New Hampshire and Maine, and into the backcountry of New England, up the Connecticut River to western Massachusetts and Vermont. Small colonies of Yankees established themselves even further afield in Newark, New Jersey, the Wyoming Valley of Pennsylvania, and Long Island, New York.[27] The principal reason for this migration was want of arable land. The most fertile lands were along the coast and up the river valleys, and most of this was occupied early on. For those families who moved into the hilly backcountry, thin soils were depleted quickly, and within a couple of generations substantial environmental degradation forced the abandonment of many hilltop farms and villages. One ubiquitous anecdote from the period relates how a young boy in one Massachusetts hill town was found in tears in a field. When asked what the matter was, he replied, "I can't get enough dirt to cover the corn!"[28] For those lucky enough to have sustainable farms, an overabundance of sons was often a spur to migration. Although Yankees tended to practice partible inheritance, they were loath to divide up productive farms into smaller chunks.[29] This resulted in either too many sons left sharing a single farmstead or, as was more often the case, the father underwriting his younger sons' migration to frontier regions where more abundant and much cheaper lands could be found.

By the end of the Revolutionary War, the primary destination of Yankee migration was Upstate New York.[30] Newly opened to settlement and containing some of the most fertile lands of the Northeast, the country was invaded by Yankees. Many found prosperity in the famous Genesee Valley, where wheat harvests were both greater in per acre yield and cheaper to produce than in New England. Yankees also developed what was a minor industry back home, dairying, into a major one in Upstate New York: the first successful cheese factory in the United States was opened by Yankees in Rome in 1851.[31] Yankees also founded important river towns such as Rochester, Utica, and Little Falls. Here many grew rich by using the abundant waterpower for mills and other industries such as textiles and shoemaking, and by using the recently completed Erie Canal for cheap shipping to lucrative eastern markets. By 1830, Yankees controlled the region's commerce, politics, and cultural life, much to the disgust of the original Dutch Yorkers, who disliked Yankee covetousness and moralism.[32] Nevertheless, these

"Yankee-Yorkers," as the immigrants came to be known, so dominated the life of Upstate New York that they soon referred to it as nothing less than the "Second New England."

The initial period of the Yankee Diaspora coincided with another period of great religious excitement known as the Second Great Awakening.[33] Lasting from the 1790s to the 1830s, the Awakening consisted of a series of intense religious revivals that flared periodically in several regions, including the New England states and the Yankee colonies in the West. The New England phase of the revival played out over the 1790s and probably had its roots, at least in part, in the profound social changes sweeping the newly constituted nation. Republicanism was the order of the day, with its ethos of egalitarianism threatening the old social hierarchies; economic activity was intensifying, drawing more and more people into the competitive individualism of the market; and the new guarantees of religious freedom led to the proliferation of religious movements and the growth of such popular sects as the Methodists and Baptists. Ministers of the established denominations, especially Congregationalists and Presbyterians, still fearing the loss of New England's chosen status, looked on in alarm. The immediate result was a succession of local revivals energetically fomented by Congregationalist and Presbyterian ministers in Maine, New Hampshire, Massachusetts, and Connecticut. Of more lasting importance, however, was the fact that these ministers harnessed this new religious fervor to shore up what they perceived to be the crumbling social order. They promoted a plethora of voluntaristic missionary, benevolent, and moral reform movements to which the people of New England responded enthusiastically with both money and time. The range of activities was truly astounding: missionary societies targeted unchurched western settlers, Native Americans, and peoples in foreign lands; tract and Bible societies sought to provide every household, no matter how poor, with religious materials; and societies of all kinds promoted anti-slavery, anti-dueling, Sabbatarianism, world peace, temperance, health, prison and educational reform, and women's rights. So dense did these reform organizations become that later observers joked that they formed a kind of Yankee "Benevolent Empire."

The revivals of the Second Great Awakening came later to the Yankees of Upstate New York, but when they did come in the 1820s and 1830s, the revival fires burned so intensely that the region has been known as the "Burned-

Over District" ever since. Here, revivalists such as Charles Grandison Finney preached a theology more suited to the optimistic individualism of the rising generation of Yankees and were rewarded by spectacular surges in church membership. A pervasive culture of aggressive evangelicalism arose in the region, as did a belief in the imminent dawn of the Millennium. As with their New England counterparts, these revivalists also channeled their audience's energies into a raft of social causes, so that, like New England, the Burned-Over District became a source of reform movements. Unlike New England, however, these "Yankee-Yorkers" tended to be more radical than their more conservative cousins back home, perhaps because of the rawness and unsettled nature of life on the New York frontier. At times, Yankee-Yorker revivalism and reformism shaded into an extremism that contemporaries termed "ultraism." This willingness to invest social causes with high emotions would define the denizens of the Burned-Over District throughout the antebellum period. Yankee-Yorkers also tended to be more religiously experimental than New England Yankees. While most associated with the mainstream denominations, others were attracted to such radically new religious movements as Millerism, Mormonism, and Spiritualism—all of which originated with Yankees in the Burned-Over District of Upstate New York. These "double distilled" Yankees, as one writer called Yankee-Yorkers, would bring an interesting leaven to the mass of Yankees now moving into the Northwest.[34]

Yankee Immigration to the Northwest Territories

As early as 1788, a Yankee settlement company had founded Marietta on the banks of the Ohio River, the first Yankee town in the Northwest Terri-tories. Next, the Western Reserve district of northeastern Ohio—a territory once claimed by Connecticut—began to fill up with Yankees from that New England state beginning in the 1790s. Yankee immigration accelerated after the turn of the century. The pushes and pulls of immigration were many. More New England farmers recognized the exhausted fertility of their lands and made the difficult decision to move on, especially since competition from farmers in the West led to falling prices for grain in New England. In addition, long winters and a generally unpredictable climate stimulated Western migration from New England after 1815 and then again during the

1830s and 1840s. New York Yankees migrated in even greater numbers for many of the same reasons. Land foreclosures in the Genesee Country of Upstate New York forced many Yankees to move on, as did the perennial problem of providing land for too many sons in a region with a growing land shortage.[35] The most salient "pull" was, of course, the availability of cheap lands, but the fact that the federal government had already provided for the political machinery necessary to convert these western lands into states also facilitated migration. In 1787, Congress passed the Northwest Ordinance establishing the Northwest Territory, a huge tract of land lying north of the Ohio River and bounded on the west by the Mississippi River. The Ordinance called for the orderly sale of the lands of this region and for the appointment of a territorial governor, a secretary, and three judges. When a section of the territory achieved a population of five thousand voting citizens, they could then elect a territorial legislature with a nonvoting representative in Congress; when the section reached a population of sixty thousand, it could apply for statehood. The Ordinance, largely the work of two Yankees, Rufus Putnam and Manasseh Cutler,[36] also called for state support of religion and education, and the banning of slavery. Eventually, six states—Ohio, Illinois, Indiana, Michigan, Wisconsin, and a part of Minnesota—were carved out of the region (in time the region came to be known as the "Old" Northwest to differentiate it from the Pacific Northwest).

While Yankee migration west was prompted primarily by economic reasons, some Yankees read larger national and even cosmic implications into their move. Yankees were relative latecomers to the Northwest. Before 1830, Upland Southerners predominated in the southern part of the region (primarily southern Ohio, southern Indiana, and southern Illinois), and when Yankees began to migrate into the region they were likely to encounter Southerners, often for the first time. Yankees were not impressed: Southerners, they felt, were poor and slovenly farmers, lazy, improvident, morally lax, given to brawling and drunkenness, and corrupted by the evils of slavery. Poverty especially offended Yankees, believing as they did in "a fixed and inevitable law, ignorance is allied with poverty, and intelligence with wealth."[37] In addition, the fundamental institutions of any well-ordered society—church, school, and civil government—were, they felt, conspicuously lacking. As unfair as this assessment actually was, Yankees nevertheless were convinced that if Southern culture were allowed to reign in the

Northwest, the result would be uncontrollable social chaos that would infect the rest of the nation and ultimately undermine the new Republic.[38] The Northwest, therefore, needed to be redeemed from the South. To accomplish this, the leading men of New England urgently called for a "crusade to extend Yankee culture."[39] Individual Yankee settlers were urged to "mingle freely and unsuspiciously with [their] neighbors, and . . . strive to bring up their habits, by successful example, to the New England standard." Thus would "the process of assimilation to New England tastes and the conquest of New England principles" be affected, "until their complete triumph [had] been made certain throughout the Northwest." And once the Northwest was won, the process would be extended to other regions of the country. One Boston merchant looked forward to the time when "New England institutions [were] established from the [Great] lakes to the Pacific, and every six miles [one would] find a New England village, with its church spires pointing to the skies and the school by its side."[40] Southern culture would simply be melted away by the application of "that all-pervading solvent and amalgam, the universal Yankee nation."[41] A Boston journalist even proposed, perhaps a bit tongue in cheek, that the name "United States" be replaced by "Yankeedonia" or "Yankeedom."[42] Of course, this kind of thinking generated a backlash among Southerners, giving rise to such ethnic slurs as being "Yankeed" (cheated) and "Yankeed over" (sold shoddy goods).[43]

In addition to their negative view of Southern culture, some Yankees perceived an equally menacing threat to the Northwest: Roman Catholicism. The region already had a population of French Canadian Catholics, and more Catholics, primarily Irish and German, were immigrating there every year. In *A Plea for the West* (1835) Congregationalist minister Lyman Beecher argued that these were merely the advanced guard of a larger "invasion," since the entire Mississippi Valley was the target of nothing less than a fantastic papal plot to create a Catholic kingdom at the United States' backdoor. Beecher exhorted his fellow Yankees to combat such designs by contributing to even greater missionary efforts and by establishing western educational institutions superior to those of the Catholics. The Northwest, Beecher believed, was to be the scene of a cosmic struggle between good and evil, between "superstition" and "evangelical light."[44] Such "nativist" or anti-Catholic sentiments had run deep with the Puritans, and these prejudices were easy to revive in their Yankee descendents. Indeed, tensions between Yankees and Catholics in the Midwest would last well into the twentieth century.

Ultimately, the coincidence of the Second Great Awakening with Yankee migration into the territories wrought a fundamental change in the Yankee concept of chosenness. Buoyed by both religious revival and territorial expansion, Yankees began to rethink the nature of New England's covenant with God. As the historian Robert Abzug put it, they slowly began "transferring a sense of chosenness from New England to the United States" at large.[45] By linking economic migration into the Northwest with larger projects of Yankee national hegemony and spiritual combat against Catholics, Yankees—confident that they were special people on a mission from God— brought an energy and purpose into the Northwest that would allow them to impact the region out of all proportion to their actual numbers.

Yankees Come to Michigan

At one time, it seemed as though all New England was coming. The immigration fever pervaded almost every hamlet of New England and "Michigania" was a very popular song in the east.

—Silas Farmer, *History of Detroit and Wayne County and Early Michigan*, 1890

Yankee immigration to Michigan was slow at first. The few that did migrate came in pursuit of commercial opportunities fueled by the fur trade, and all settled in one of Michigan's only two population centers, Detroit or Mackinac Island. Before the War of 1812, two Yankees, Solomon Sibley of Massachusetts and Stephen Mack of Connecticut, had established shops in Detroit. Other Yankees were brought to Detroit during their Army service and stayed on once hostilities ceased. Detroit was also regularly visited by the ubiquitous Yankee peddler, who, with his clocks, tin ware, and other notions, was a familiar sight in the Northwest Territories. Farther north, John Jacob Astor's American Fur Company drew a few Yankees to its Mackinac Island outpost. Vermonter Gurdon Saltonstall Hubbard and Massachusetts-born Rix Robinson both entered into Astor's employ in 1818 and served as clerks and factors. Hubbard would eventually migrate to Chicago, where he grew rich as a meat packer and merchant, while Robinson would remain in

Michigan, marry an Ottawa woman, and become instrumental in the development of the Grand River Valley and prominent in local politics.[46]

Michigan's public lands were put on sale by the U.S. government in 1818. Despite this, two factors slowed large-scale Yankee migration: the lack of easy transportation to the territory and the lack of good information about the quality of Michigan's agricultural land. The route through Ohio was difficult because of the infamous Black Swamp; overland across Ontario was slow and arduous; and traveling by ship across Lake Erie from Buffalo was expensive, unreliable, and dangerous. In 1818, however, the first regular steamship service was opened to Detroit, followed in 1825 by the opening of the Erie Canal in Upstate New York.[47] Both served to facilitate travel and lower the cost substantially; by the 1820s, deck passage across Lake Erie cost only three dollars, making the overall cost of travel from Massachusetts about ten dollars. Freight rates fell such that Yankee immigrants were encouraged to bring all their belongings with them.[48] Travel time, too, was considerably shortened. Before the opening of the canal, it took thirty-two days to reach Michigan's interior from Vermont. By 1835, the interior of Michigan could be reached from New England in as little as three weeks.[49] As one historian put it, "The opening of the Erie Canal acted like an open sluiceway to drain off the population of New England."[50] The canal also facilitated a substantial migration to Michigan of Yankee-Yorkers, those Yankees who had already established themselves for a generation in Upstate New York.

An accurate estimate of Michigan's agricultural potential also took time to develop. Yankees were always strategic planners, and rarely would they launch themselves into the wilderness without advance knowledge that conditions ahead were conducive to success.[51] Unfortunately, the earliest surveying expeditions barely made it beyond the pale of Detroit, and these erroneously reported that all of the Lower Peninsula was either swampy or sandy. Based on a survey of Jackson County in 1815, for example, a government report concluded that in Michigan's interior, "not more than one acre in a hundred, or perhaps in a thousand, could be cultivated."[52] It was not until 1818 that surveys disclosed the true nature of the land, thus piquing Yankee interest. Yankees were especially enthusiastic about the frequency in southwestern Michigan of what the surveyors called "oak barrens," but what they called "oak openings," thinly timbered prairies ideal for farmsteads. Forests were also abundant, as were numerous waterways that "caused Yankee eyes to gleam with visions of mills, canals, and steamboats."[53] It took a while for news of the land's richness to reach the Northeast, first by letters and newspaper articles, and then in maps and guidebooks.[54] The most popular of these were the maps of John Farmer, an early surveyor from Upstate New York who had the foresight to copyright his Michigan maps and offer them for sale in 1826, the year after the opening of the Erie Canal. In 1830, he combined the maps with a detailed gazetteer published as *Farmer's Guide to Michigan*. From then on, few Yankee immigrants would head west to Michigan without a copy of *Farmer's* in their pocket.[55] By the early 1820s, Yankees had slowly begun to settle the counties close to Detroit: Washtenaw, Lenawee, and Hillsdale. After the opening of the Erie Canal and the publication of *Farmer's* and other guidebooks, waves of Yankees filled in the southern three tiers of counties from Monroe on Lake Erie to Berrien on Lake Michigan.[56] Those who followed the newly opened Chicago Road settled the southern tier of counties, while another stream of Yankees followed the Territorial Road, opened in 1834, and settled the second and third tiers of counties.[57]

Patterns of Yankee Settlement

Our national mythology often portrays frontier settlement as the work of solitary individuals and families hacking a living out of the wilderness miles from any neighbor. In many cases this was true, but in terms of the Yankee Diaspora, patterns of settlement were more varied and complex. In many counties of Lower Michigan, for instance, the first Yankees on the ground were surveyors and land speculators. The Land Ordinance of 1785 had rejected as too chaotic the "Southern system" of land alienation, in which government land was purchased and then surveyed. Instead, it adopted the more orderly "New England system," in which government land was surveyed into townships six miles square in advance of sale.[58] Therefore, before the government could sell the public lands of Michigan, the land had to be surveyed. Many ambitious young men—men such as Lucius Lyon and John Farmer—were lured to the territory as members of survey teams, and, since they had first look and knew the best lands, many became active land speculators, buying up large tracts for future sale at higher prices. Lyon, for example, owned land in no fewer than twenty Michigan counties over the course of his career.[59] Still other Yankees were sent to Michigan as agents of land companies that sought to speculate in government lands. Although land speculators in their day were often vilified and accused of causing financial panics and fluctuations in the economy, they nevertheless staked their success on the economic development of their region. They therefore served an invaluable role in bringing investment money into the territory, thus promoting community development and the creation of commercial infrastructure as a by-product of their pursuit of personal financial gain.[60]

The majority of Yankees, however, did not come to Michigan as individual speculators. Following precedents set in earlier phases of the Yankee Diaspora into the New England backcountry and into Upstate New York, Yankees came in planned migrations, employing organized groups such as colonization companies or covenanted communities, or as groups of families through what is known as "chain migration."

Colonization Companies

New Englanders were among the few immigrant groups that consisted of "highly organized groups that deliberately moved and settled in such a way as to preserve identity."[61] Even at this late date, some Yankees still strongly retained the old Puritan community spirit and desire for social cohesion. Typically, a number of families from a specific village or neighborhood desirous of migrating would create a colonization company in order to facilitate the re-creation out west of the New England village life to which they were used accustomed.[62] Such companies designated leaders who would draw up a compact spelling out the financial and moral requirements of members, as well as dictating the physical layout of the colony. Company leaders would also be in charge of collecting funds and organizing the advance scouting for lands. Once suitable lands had been located and purchased, lots would be drawn to distribute farm and village lots, and then the company would begin to migrate as individual families or groups of families. The first Yankee settlement in the Northwest, Marietta, Ohio (1788), was the result of such a company, and the practice of organized Yankee colonization continued until the Civil War.

We can identify several Michigan settlements that had their origins in these organized mass migrations. In 1817, a company from Royalston, Massachusetts, settled on government land at the confluence of the Macon and

John Ball, Yankee Speculator

John Ball is an ideal example of the shrewd Yankee land agent and speculator. Born in Hebron, New Hampshire, in 1794, Ball developed into an exceedingly restless spirit. After taking a degree from Dartmouth College in 1820 and studying the law for two years, he embarked on several sea voyages taking him to the American South and the South Seas, superintended for a time an oil cloth factory in Upstate New York, and traveled across the continent on the Oregon Trail to the Willamette Valley, where he farmed for a time before returning to Upstate New York to practice law in Troy. Soon bored with the law, Ball jumped at the chance in 1836 to do some "land looking" out West in Michigan for a New York land syndicate. On his second trip to Michigan, he was told to investigate the Grand River Valley for suitable investment lands. There he purchased a tract of valuable pine forest and settled for good in Grand Rapids. Despite the onset of economic depression in 1837, Ball continued to speculate successfully in government lands and opened a law firm to facilitate his work as a land broker. His methods were simple: "We had a fair legal business in our office, and I had other land agency business, after the sale of the state lands, so that I began to accumulate something. I operated in wild lands, commencing with the pay for my services for selecting these lands, selling at low rates when opportunity presented, knowing where I could reinvest to advantage" (Ball 1994, 111). In time, Ball's land speculation allowed him to branch out into city real estate and manufacturing, and he became a rich and respected citizen, devoting much of his later years to the typically Yankee promotion of education, scientific agriculture, and traveling for pleasure. Fittingly enough, before he died at the ripe old age of ninety, Ball willed forty acres of prime land to the city of Grand Rapids for use as the public park that bears his name to this day.

Raisin Rivers, although ownership disputes with the local Indians induced the colonists to move on. Eventually, remnants of the company founded the town of Blissfield, Lenawee County, in 1824. The heyday of colonization companies in Michigan came in the boom years of the early 1830s. In 1830, for example, a colony from Windsor, Vermont, settled Prairie Ronde in Kalamazoo County; Vermont colonies also founded Schoolcraft, Sylvan, and Bennington. Three years later, Rhode Islander Samuel Dexter led a company of sixty-three Yankee-Yorkers to Ionia County, where the colonists named the village of Dexter in his honor. Three years later, a similar group in Upstate New York confederated as the "Rochester Company." Given warrant to inspect lands in Ohio, Indiana, and Michigan, the company's agents chose Duplain Township in the northeast corner of Michigan's Clinton County as the most advantageous to agricultural success and most like the country they would be leaving. The Rochester colonists founded the village of Mapleton, which centered on a sawmill and a gristmill.[63] To this day, the area around Mapleton is still referred to as "The Colony."

Covenanted Communities

Yankee colonization companies sought to reproduce in the West culturally homogenous communities that shared ethnic and religious values all in the service of economic gain. Occasionally, the religious element predominated, and Yankees sought to move as intact church congregations. Such colonization companies have come to be known as "covenanted communities."[64] The towns of Romeo (1827), Vermontville (1837), and Olivet (1844) all started as Congregationalist communities, with Vermontville perhaps the best documented.[65] In the fall of 1835, a Congregationalist minister from East Poultney, Vermont, the Reverend Sylvester Cochrane, traveled to Michigan in search of an established community suitable for the relocation of his church. Finding none, Rev. Cochrane returned to Vermont with the idea of creating his own Michigan community by constituting a colonization company in which religion would be at least as important as economic betterment. Rev. Cochrane convoked several meetings in various Vermont towns to see if he could interest enough families in the enterprise, and on March 27, 1836, in Castleton, Vermont, forty-two heads of households signed the Union Colony Constitution and pledged to migrate to Michigan. The Union Colony Constitution had several of the standard colonization company articles, but it also included an explicit statement that the purpose of the colony was "to form ourselves into such a community as will enable us to enjoy the same social and religious privileges which we leave behind."[66] In furtherance of this goal, the constitution called for the immediate creation of a church and school, the banning of "ardent spirits," and a rigid observance of the Sabbath by both man and beast.

Three Union Colony agents were immediately dispatched to Michigan, where they bought a large tract of government land in Eaton County. Here they platted a village to be called Vermontville. It was to be an ideal New England village with a main square around which church, school, and township hall would be built, and with home lots laid out along north-south and east-west axes. Only about half of the original signers of the Union Colony Constitution ever migrated to Vermontville, but despite the village's slow growth, the colonizers stayed true to their original intentions of founding a godly community. In the winter of 1837, Rev. Cochrane organized the Vermontville Congregational Church and records indicate that only two of the colonists failed to become members, and this because of moral lapses. School was started the following year in a log schoolhouse. Next, an "academical association" (i.e., a high school) was formed in 1843, and a headmaster, the Reverend W. U. Benedict, appointed to oversee its operation. Eventually, the academy would attract scholars from much of Eaton County and beyond.

In the first years of the Union Colony, coordination between township, church, and school was tight, and spiritual discipline strict. Such fervor was hard to maintain, though, and while "few non New England elements were introduced into the community . . . the religious zeal declined."[67] The Reverend Cochrane left to take up another Congregationalist pulpit after five years, and an earlier controversy over the academy, in 1839, had already led to schism and the creation of a Methodist Church in Vermontville. Nevertheless, the colony retained for decades an air of religious seriousness and purpose often lacking in other Michigan settlements. According to one pioneer looking back over his Vermontville childhood, on the Sabbath not even a "loud smile" was permitted.[68]

Chain Migration

Yankee colonization companies and covenanted communities are the most famous aspects of Yankee migration to Michigan, but they were in fact not the norm. Among the first generation of Yankee and Yankee-Yorker migrants, most came as separate nuclear families determined to carve out a family farm.[69] Typically, a Yankee farmer who wished to migrate to Michigan would first come out alone in order to locate and buy suitable land. Yankee farmers sought land with high clay content, and for this reason they tended to settle in the counties below the sandy pinelands north of the Grand Valley. New Englanders also preferred forestlands that reminded them of home. As mentioned above, they especially prized oak openings, although they soon learned the advantages of the open prairies of southwestern Michigan. Once land was purchased, and a rudimentary shack or lean-to constructed, the farmer would return east to retrieve his family and possessions.[70] If he had chosen well, a farmer might hope to have a prosperous farm within a few years of migration, and he could also hope to have familiar neighbors soon. Since Yankees were inveterate letter writers, invariably a Yankee settler would write back home extolling the virtues of his new farmstead. This would often induce relations or neighbor families from back in New England or Upstate New York to make the move themselves. Even more than colonization companies and covenanted communities, such "chain migration" accounts for why Yankee migrants from the same neighborhood or state tended to settle near to each other, forming close-knit Yankee communities in Michigan.[71] Thus we find concentrations of Massachusetts-born settlers in and around Detroit and Kalamazoo, Yankee-Yorkers in Lenawee County, and Vermonters in Wayne, Oakland, Washtenaw, Macomb, and Kent Counties. We also find high concentrations of migrants from both Massachusetts and Connecticut in Berrien County.[72] Of all the methods of migration, "chain migration" accounts for most of the Yankee population in Michigan.

However they arrived, the migration of Yankees and Yankee-Yorkers in the 1830s and 1840s drastically changed the demographics of the Michigan Territory and dramatically hastened its development. Historical demographers tell us that, according to the 1850 census, Michigan had the highest percentage (45%) and absolute number (179,703) of Yankee and Yankee-Yorker settlers of any Midwestern state, and that "[t]here were more Yankee natives than Michigan natives in Michigan" by that time.[73] The census records also indicate that most Yankees settled in the fifteen counties of the south central portion of the state, precisely those that had the geography and climate most similar to southern New England and Upstate New York. These counties are Barry, Branch, Calhoun, Clinton, Eaton, Hillsdale, Ingham, Ionia, Jackson, Kalamazoo, Lenawee, Livingston, St. Joseph, Shiawassee, and Washtenaw. All of these counties were first organized in response to the flood of Yankees in the 1830s.[74]

Yankees and the Early Government of Michigan

On January 11, 1805, President Thomas Jefferson signed the act creating the Territory of Michigan. Assuming that Michigan would be in the lateral zone of New England colonization, Jefferson appointed predominately New England men of his own party, the Democratic Republicans, to positions of authority in the new territorial government. General William Hull was selected to be the first governor, but, in the wake of his ignominious surrender of Detroit to the British during the War of 1812, Hull was replaced by Lewis Cass of New Hampshire.[75] Cass was an excellent choice. During his eighteen years as governor (1813 to 1831), he tirelessly promoted Michigan's development, lobbying Congress for funds and taking it upon himself to personally survey the conditions of the territory. Cass also wholeheartedly supported the speedy creation of representative government in Michigan, a cause especially popular among Michigan's Yankee population.[76] During his long career, Cass would serve twelve years in Congress as a senator, run for president, and end his career as secretary of state under Buchanan. In the decades before the Civil War, Lewis Cass was the face of Michigan to the nation. "Little wonder," writes Stewart Holbrook, "settlers named their babies for him, as well as a county, a river, and a town."[77]

Hull and Cass were only two of the many Yankees who controlled Michigan's territorial and early state government. When Congress finally granted representative government to Michigan in 1823, the governor, the territorial secretary, the congressional delegate, the four judges of the Supreme Court, and most of the Territorial Council were New Englanders.[78] From then until well after the Civil War, Yankees continued to play prominent roles in state politics. Between 1805 and 1870, twelve out of fifteen governors were Yankees, and at the local level during the same period, nearly 77 percent of all officeholders in the south central portion of the state were of New England descent.[79] In practical terms, what this meant was that Yankees had the opportunity to influence Michigan with many Yankee-inspired legal and governmental institutions. For example, many of the territorial statutes and almost all of Michigan's probate law were taken from Massachusetts, and a law specifying public whipping as punishment for certain crimes came directly from Vermont.[80] Perhaps most tellingly, Michigan "became the first western state to adopt the township system and its attendant forum, the town

meeting."[81] Townships were modeled on the New England town, which was
not a town in the modern sense of a small settlement, but a land grant made
to the earliest Puritan colonists.[82] The right of the township to govern itself
through the democratic town meeting had been jealously guarded by the
Puritans and later became a badge of Yankee pride. In reality, Michigan adopted the hybrid form of local government found in New York that subsumes
the township within the county. It is notable, though, that townships were
organized in Michigan long before county governments came into being, and
that they continue to this day to be the bedrock of the state's government—a
monument to "the New England instinct for self government."[83]

Yankees and the Earlier Inhabitants of Michigan

While the Yankee population came to dominate Michigan for a time, they
did not, of course, find the territory unoccupied. Here they would encounter Native Americans, French *habitants,* and, in the extreme southwest of
the state, white Upland Southerners who had earlier migrated north from
Ohio and Indiana, as well as a few freed or fugitive African-American slaves.
Yankee attitudes toward these previous inhabitants were complex, but all
were marked by the Yankee sense of cultural superiority and cultural mission. On the whole, Yankees preferred to interact with other Yankees and
not with "foreigners," which to them meant all of those not of New England
descent.[84] Despite this, like it or not, Yankees felt duty-bound to bring their
neighbors, whether Native American, French, or Southern, up to "the New
England standard." Nothing less than the fate of Michigan, the Northwest,
and the nation depended on it.

Yankees and Native Americans

Throughout the Yankee Diaspora, from the Great Lakes to the Oregon Territory to Hawaii and beyond, a similar contest played out during the frontier
period between Yankee traders and Yankee missionaries. Concerned with
profits, the traders arrived to exploit natural resources, and they eagerly
used Native peoples as their workforce. Concerned with souls, missionaries
followed, and they were just as eager to save Native peoples from what they
considered the less virtuous aspects of Yankee civilization by converting
them to Christianity and assimilating them to western ways. Hardly passive

victims in this process, Native peoples nevertheless found themselves caught between the competing imperatives of Yankee culture: the creation of wealth and the imposition of Yankee notions of the ideal social order. In hindsight, it is hard to say which was more destructive to Native cultures.

Yankee missionaries began arriving in Michigan as early as 1820. As mentioned previously, the Second Great Awakening unleashed a flood of efforts to evangelize the world, including the creation of such agencies as the American Board of Commissioners for Foreign Missions (ABCFM), organized by Presbyterians and Congregationalists in Boston in 1810. In 1823, under the auspices of the ABCFM, the Reverend William Ferry and his wife Amanda opened a mission on Mackinac Island, then the hub of the northern fur trade and headquarters of the American Fur Company.[85] Here, they gathered a Presbyterian congregation, built a church in the New England style (the oldest still extant in Michigan), and established a boarding school for Chippewa and Métis children. The goal of the mission was to spread evangelical Christianity and to prepare the local children for life as citizens in the American Republic through both academic and vocational education. Between 1822 and 1837, the ABCFM sent approximately forty missionaries to the Mackinaw Mission—all but three of whom hailed from either New England or Upstate New York.[86] New England Baptists as well targeted Michigan Indians involved in the fur trade. The Baptist Board of Foreign Missions, also located in Boston, established the Niles Carey Mission in 1822, the Thomas Station Mission near Grand Rapids in 1827, and the Sault Ste. Marie Mission the following year. Each was staffed by a married couple devoted to the twin tasks of Native conversion to evangelical Protestantism and cultural assimilation along New England lines.[87] In the end, none of these Calvinist missions were conspicuously successful, especially when compared to the successes of Roman Catholic missions in the area. Perhaps this was because, as one historian put it of a Baptist missionary in the Upper Peninsula, "He had gone to people of the forest, whose entire life was a struggle against nature, with a God too stern to accept."[88] Despite this, New England missionary societies would continue to sponsor Indian missions in Michigan until the 1850s.[89]

Lay Yankee attitudes toward Michigan's Native Americans were more mixed. On the one hand, many Yankee settlers found their Indian neighbors to be invaluable trading partners integral to their success as pioneers.[90] Of course, non-Yankees were quick to point out that this was an unequal

Old Mission Church built by Rev. William Ferry on Mackinac Island, Michigan. (Courtesy of Western Michigan University Archives and Regional History Collections.)

relationship, and that "our sharp, shrewd settlers from New York and New England were not very scrupulous in their dealings with those upon whose good will they were so dependent."[91] Yet, many a Yankee family formed close relations with Native families, occasionally intermarrying (e.g., Rix Robinson), and, in the spirit of Roger Williams, some Yankees were genuinely concerned that Indian rights be respected.

On the other hand, conditioned by generations of Indian warfare, most recently the War of 1812, other Yankees mirrored the national mood that Native Americans were unassimilable and an obstacle to the settlement of the Northwest. Only expulsion further west or detention on reservations would solve "the Indian problem." As the *Detroit Gazette* opined in 1820, only then could "the red children of the forest . . . partake of the comforts and blessings of civilized life" and learn the skills "that would do honor to a citizen of Massachusetts or Connecticut."[92] Michigan governor Lewis Cass, who engineered many of the treaties that dispossessed Native Americans of their Michigan lands, was more brutal in his assessment of Native Americans. In an 1827 article for the *North American Review,* he compared them to wild animals: "Like the bear, and deer, and buffalo, an Indian lives as his father lived . . . in a succession of listless indolence and vigorous exertion to provide for his animal wants or to gratify his baleful passions." Such "a barbarous people," Cass later wrote, "cannot live in contact with a civilized community."[93] Such sentiments dovetailed with the U.S. policy then current, and by 1840 the vast majority of Michigan's Native peoples had either been confined to reservations or exiled beyond the Mississippi. Some Yankees lamented this injustice, but most saw it as inevitable and only a few tried to stop it.[94]

The conflicting nature of Yankee attitudes toward the Native Americans was frequently embodied in the same person. This is perhaps best illustrated by the life and work of Henry R. Schoolcraft.[95] A Yankee-Yorker, Schoolcraft was born in Albany County, New York, in 1793. He was educated in New England, attending Middlebury College, where he studied geology and mineralogy. After graduation, Schoolcraft headed west to explore the mineral resources of Missouri and Arkansas. This experience led him to an appointment as cartographer and government agent stationed on Lake Superior. At this remote outpost, Schoolcraft became fascinated by Native American culture and began his lifelong study of what today we call ethnology. From 1836 to 1841, he served as superintendent of Indian affairs in Michigan, charged with negotiating several significant treaties. Schoolcraft's duties gave him abundant opportunities to record Indian customs and practices, myths, and legends. A prolific writer whose work inspired Longfellow's *Hiawatha*, Schoolcraft's crowning achievement was the six-volume *Historical and Statistical Information Respecting the History, Condition, and Prospects of the Indian Tribes of the United States* (1851–1857), still respected by scholars today as an invaluable source on early nineteenth-century Indian life. Schoolcraft's sympathy for Native culture is evident in the loving care with which he recorded it, and in the fact that he married a Chippewa woman in 1822. Despite this, Schoolcraft shared in his contemporaries' pessimistic and self-serving assumption that the Indians were a "vanishing people" fated to be crushed by the weight of Yankee civilization. He, too, believed that segregation was the only answer: looking back in 1857, Schoolcraft wrote, "Whatever may have been the sentiments of humanitarians, . . . no practicable prospect of their reclamation and restoration to society was presented, . . . except in their total separation from the evils surrounding them . . . on the territory specially appropriated for their use, where, under the operation of their own laws and institutions, their better qualities might develop themselves."[96] Such was the price of Yankee progress.

Yankees and French *Habitants*

Yankee attitudes toward the French *habitants* were more straightforwardly negative than those toward Native Americans, and this for several reasons. While the Indians came by their lack of civilization naturally, the French were ostensibly civilized Europeans who had allowed themselves to fall into a state of barbarism and thus were culpable for their failings. While Native religions were dismissed out of hand by Yankees, the French were deeply Roman Catholic and therefore seen as formidable foes in the contest for control of the West. So notorious nationally was Michigan Yankees' disdain for French *habitant* culture that later in the century Orlando Bolivar Wilcox, using the pseudonym "Walter March," wrote *Shoepac Recollections* (1856), a moderately successful novel satirizing the discontent of the judgmental "Bostonians" when faced with the "carefree French" in 1830s Detroit. A shoe-pac is part shoe and part moccasin, and thus an excellent symbol of "the blending of European and Indian culture" so despised by Yankees.[97]

In addition to the contest of cultures, we should bear in mind historic reasons for Yankee antipathy toward *habitants*. Throughout the colonial period, New England had been at war with French Canada, and the violence of this conflict had left deep and lasting scars that exacerbated New Englanders' long-standing distrust of the French nation. Settling in an area once controlled by the French and their Indian allies, therefore, must have seemed to Francophobic Yankees like entering the lion's den. It is interesting to note that one of the more popular village names in Michigan was Deerfield. The original Deerfield was founded in seventeenth-century western Massachusetts and had been subjected to numerous devastating attacks by the French and their Indian allies over the years. Perhaps the fact that the Massachusetts Deerfield managed to survive such onslaughts made the name a reliable talisman in the face of Michigan's entrenched French Canadian culture.[98] Finally, as the *habitants* more easily adapted to the market economy than did the Native Americans, Michigan's French Canadians often became economic rivals of the Yankees. Famous is the tale of bitter friction between *habitant* Louis Campau and Yankee Lucius Lyon, both of whom sought to control the development of Grand Rapids. Whereas Lyon platted his portion of the city at right angles to the river, Campau, in an effort to block access from Lyon's plat, platted his contiguous portion on the diagonal, thus creating the bizarre traffic patterns that afflict downtown Grand Rapids to this day.[99] Although

Yankees in French Detroit, from Walter March, *Shoepac Recollections*, 1856

[A]s settlers from New England began to thicken among us . . . it gradually came to light that our lively little community were scarce a grain better than the wicked, nay than the very heathen; witness the fiddling and dancing on Sunday evenings (and pleasant Sunday evenings they were deemed by us, in our dreadful ignorance), wherever there was any little neighborhood of French people—on the great wide porch, or beneath trees on the grass; or, if in the house, with the doors and windows thrown wide open. And there were the prettiest and most mischievous-eyed French girls, dancing away for dear life with the good-looking, frankmannered voyajeurs, or courreurs de bois, in their red, yellow, or green sashes, long black hair, and blue calico shirts. Such abominations attracted the "growing attention" of the strict sober-sides from the land of Jonathan Edwards, as he passed these dens of Apollyon, on his way to the place where prayer was wont to be made. Then was there not racing to church the year round, and racing home again? And were there not regular trotting matches on the afternoons of the great days of the church, which brought the people in from the country, up and down the river? Especially, was there ever anything like it in the winter season, when the wicked river would even wink at these atrocities by freezing over, so that nothing was seen on Sunday afternoons but carioles turned up in front, in a curl like a skate, gliding, or rather flying, over the ice, two and two? . . . Then on Easter morning, was not the church-yard of St. Ann's fairly riotous with boys cracking painted eggs? Nay, in the same precincts, were not idolatries frequently committed? Was not the Host carried in procession by chanting Jesuits and nuns, to a high mound called Mount Calvary, where there was a huge cross, and beneath which lay the tomb of our Saviour? Doubt not that these abominations smelt in the nostrils of the sons of the Puritans.

Michigan's French *habitants* were never so numerous that they managed to create a Creole culture as vibrant as, for example, that found in Louisiana, they persisted nevertheless—and this in the face of relentless Yankee dismissiveness and cultural imperialism. As with the Native Americans, Yankees had a tendency to underestimate the adaptiveness and tenacity of their French Canadian neighbors.

Yankees and White Southerners

Among the earliest American settlers in Southwest Michigan were white Upland Southerners (Yankee attitudes toward African Americans will be discussed in a later chapter). As one local historian put it so colorfully, when Yankees "reached the counties of St. Joseph, Cass, Berrien, Kalamazoo, and Van Buren, they found themselves preceded by the adventurous successors of Daniel Boone and his Coadjutors, who having crossed the Cumberland and Alleghany Mountains, had spread themselves over Kentucky, Tennessee, Ohio, Indiana, and Illinois, and following the track of Gen. Wayne, this advance army of civilization had established their pickets in these counties, picking out the choicest portions of the country."[100] Attracted by the prairie lands of southern Michigan, these white Southern settlers followed the Chicago Trail up from Fort Wayne across the Michigan border, where they created several centers with a Southern flavor. Virginia Corners was founded on Prairie Ronde by Basil Harrison in 1829. Harrison was born in Frederick County, Maryland, spent his childhood in Virginia and Pennsylvania, and then migrated to Kentucky, Ohio, and finally to Michigan. The major city of Berrien County, Niles, was founded by three Southern families up from Richmond, Indiana, in 1829.[101] LaGrange and Ontwa, Cass County, were also notable for their strong Southern roots.[102]

So different were these white Upland Southern settlers from the newly arrived Yankees in terms of lifestyle, religion, and politics, that "two differing political and social cultures were created within the state."[103] Political historian Ronald Formisano tells us that in Howard Township, Cass County, "the early settlers divided into 'two parties,' one called Yankees, which indiscriminately included all Easterners whether from New England or not, and 'Hoosiers,' who probably included ex-Indianans and ex-Southerners."[104] As mentioned previously, Yankees considered white Southerners rivals in the definition of the national culture, and wherever they encountered them, competition—sometimes bitter—occurred. However, the nature of the competition was different from that between Yankees and the Native Americans, French *habitants,* or African Americans. While they fought over issues ranging from slavery to the funding of public schools, Yankees always recognized that white Southerners were English descendents like themselves, and, as heirs to the same English values, they believed that white Southerners were more likely to be won over to New England principles in the end. Racial equals, Yankees tended to mix more freely with their white Southern neighbors. Warm relations between individuals and families were common, and, over the course of the nineteenth century, intermarriage became increasingly widespread.[105] Ultimately, Yankee numbers were so overwhelming in Michigan that the Southern element did not have the same lasting impact as in Ohio, Indiana, and Illinois. However, their presence did serve as a reminder to Yankees that, whatever else their individual motives might be, their settlement on the Michigan frontier was part of a far larger cultural crusade to "redeem the West" from the South.

Yankees on the Michigan Frontier

Father's farm was rescued from the wilderness and consecrated to the plow and husbandry through sweat and blood. We ofttimes encountered perils and were weary from labor, often times hungry and thirsty, often suffered from cold and heat, frequently destitute of comfortable apparel and condemned to toil as the universal doom of humanity—thus earning our bread by the sweat of our brows.

—William Nowlin, *The Bark Covered House,* 1876

Everything about the life and career of William Nowlin marks him as a typical Michigan Yankee pioneer farmer—except for the fact that near the end of his life he sat down and wrote a book about it. *The Bark Covered House* (1876) is one of the finest firsthand accounts of Yankee pioneer life in Michigan and is still a lively read even today. Nowlin relates how his father, John, barely able to compete because of the rising land prices in New York, became infected with "Michigan fever," convinced that only there could he provide for his family and find land for his children. Accordingly, in 1832 he bought eighty acres near what would become the town of Dearborn. Two years later, he transported his family down the Erie Canal and across Lake Erie to Detroit, and from here the family walked by way of the Chicago Road and an Indian trail the twelve miles to their new home. Nowlin's mother, Melinda, was not enthusiastic about what she found. Convinced that the family would either "be killed by the Indians, perish in the wilderness, or starve to death," she rued the day she ever left her comfortable home back east.[106]

Life on the Michigan frontier was just as precarious as Mrs. Nowlin feared it would be. Indeed, what comes through in painful detail in William Nowlin's memoir—written some thirty years after the fact—is that pioneering in Michigan consisted of unremitting toil and considerable physical and emotional hardship. John Nowlin's recently purchased land was, of course, completely unimproved, with no buildings and still covered with a thick forest. With the help of neighbors, the family did manage to build a rudimentary "bark covered house," the log cabin memorialized in the title of Nowlin's book. Father and son then set to work chopping trees with a vengeance, racing to get crops in the ground before winter. Potatoes and the "garden stuff" grew well, but the ground was still too shaded by the surrounding forest for a good crop of corn.[107] Food was thus scarce at first, leading to what came to be called the "Michigan Appetite," a ravenousness that could not be satisfied even when food became abundant.[108] The lack of food variety also led to such maladies as the "Michigan Rash" (beriberi) and other forms of malnutrition.[109] If this weren't bad enough, before the land was cleared and drained the Nowlins were constantly beset by literal clouds of mosquitoes droning with their "disagreeable music."[110] Malaria was common, and few of the first generation of pioneers escaped frequent, almost predictable bouts of "the shakes."[111] We might decry the waste today, but it is little wonder that Yankees so ruthlessly decimated the forests and wetlands of Michigan, associated as they were with hunger and disease. Only decades later could they look at the natural wonders about them and wax philosophical.

Michigan's Yankee pioneer farmers waged war not only against nature, but against the relentless demands of the local economy as well. The Nowlins came to Michigan primarily to get ahead in life, but prosperity did not come easily, nor was it inevitable. John Nowlin bought his land specifically to be near the markets of Detroit, but accessibility long remained a problem, with roads barely graded and almost impassable after the rains. Efficient road systems were yet to be built (as they would be eventually by the pioneers themselves), and it would be several years before the railroad arrived in the vicinity. In the meantime, crop prices remained low, and in order to produce

The Pilgrim Oak of Michigan, from William Nowlin, *The Bark Covered House*, 1876

The oak tree was more fortunate and escaped the fatal ax, a number of years after all the timber around it had been chopped and cleared away. On account of its greatness, and its having so nice a body, father let it stand as monarch of the clearing. But few came into our clearing without seeing his majesty's presence. His roots were immense. They had been centuries creeping and feeling their way along, extracting life from mother earth to sustain their gigantic body. The acorn, from which that oak grew, must have been planted long before, and the tree which grew from it have been dressed many times in its summer robe of green, and it was, doubtless, flourishing when the "Mayflower" left the English Channel. When she was slowly making her way from billow to billow, through the then almost unknown sea, bearing some of the most brave and liberty-loving men and women of the world, at that time, could produce; when the hearts of the Pilgrim Fathers were beating high with hopes of liberty and escape from tyranny, when their breath came low and short for fear of what might await them; when they landed on the American shore—yes! when that little band of pilgrims were kneeling on Plymouth Rock, and offering up thanksgiving and praise to the Almighty, who had brought them safely o'er the trackless deep, that oak was quietly standing, gathering strength to make it what it was when we came to Michigan.

the volume that would yield a profit, the Nowlins had to expand their farming operation quickly. This, of course, took money. Like most Yankee emigrants, the Nowlins did possess some financial resources when they arrived in Michigan, but not enough to avoid having to mortgage their farm in order to buy draft animals. As luck would have it, the very year John Nowlin mortgaged his farm—1837—the United States suffered a severe economic depression that hit Michigan especially hard (a second economic contraction would hit two years later). Cash money became scarce, land values dropped, and so did commodity prices. The Nowlins barely survived. William Nowlin would later record that the mortgage became "like a cancer eating up our substance, gnawing day and night." To pay it off, the family scrambled to sell whatever they could get their hands on: maple sugar, melons, honey, even their labor.[112] In desperation, William and his father turned to hunting game full time, since meat and skins were the only products that held their value in these bleak economic times. What farming they did was largely for subsistence.

Slowly, ever so slowly, the situation brightened. The mortgage debt was paid off, the Michigan economy improved, and the Nowlins grew into the prosperous farm family they had always hoped to be. By the mid-1840s, William Nowlin remembered, "the pioneer felt himself safe," free to enjoy "the fragrance of the rose and the joyful songs of civilization." William's father, now flush with cash, bought two more farms near Dearborn, built himself a substantial brick house in 1854, and, as he had always intended, provided farms for his sons. He was, by any calculation, a successful man. Yet, despite having achieved great financial rewards, John Nowlin never felt secure enough to retire. He continued to buy more land and expand his operations until the day he died in 1869. Sorely tested during his early days in Michigan, John Nowlin—even in the midst of plenty—could never escape what his son called the "example of the bees" summed up in the old Puritan maxim, "it was best to work and improve the time."[113] Such persistent anxiety over security was the psychological fate of many a first-generation Yankee pioneer farmer on the Michigan frontier.

The Yankee Farm in Michigan

As Yankees like the Nowlin family transitioned from pioneer subsistence farming to settled agriculture in Michigan, broad patterns emerged. R. L. Power, in his book, *Planting Corn Belt Culture* (1953), pointed out that Yankee farms throughout the Midwest were in many ways quite distinctive when compared to those of Upland Southerners. Upland Southerners, using the traditional metes and bounds land survey system, tended to lay out their farms in irregular shapes following the rugged topography of the Upland South, a topography that they also encountered in eastern and southern Ohio and southern Indiana. Yankees, on the other hand, constrained by the rectilinear land division imposed on the Northwest by the Land Ordinance of 1785, laid out their farms in regular squares, with the main house situated on the road and close to transportation to improve efficiency. Reflecting the colder climate of the North, barns were more prevalent on Yankee farms.

William Nowlin, for example, records that "Father wanted a frame barn very much" and he built one the minute he had the resources.[114] Other outbuildings (chicken coops, woodsheds, etc.) were also more common on Yankee farms, and the painting of all structures on the farm became *de rigueur* (usually barn red or plain white). Neatness was something of an obsession with Yankee farmers. Barnyards typically were kept swept and free of debris, and wood neatly stacked and often covered. In time, shade trees were introduced to the barnyard, as were flowerbeds and shrubs around the house.[115] Such luxuries were potent symbols for Yankees of a farmer's prosperity. Yankees were keenly aware that the appearance of their farms advertised their status and reflected their values. Indeed, the Yankee farm was a microcosmic symbol of how Yankees expected the rest of the country, if not the world, to be organized.

In terms of actual farm produce, corn was the dominant crop for Yankees in Michigan during the early years. Corn could be easily cultivated and used for food (e.g., the Yankee staple, johnnycake), for cattle and pig feed, or for distilling into easily transportable corn liquor. Very quickly, however, Yankees began the extensive cultivation of wheat, followed by a diversity of other grains such as barley, buckwheat, rye, and oats.[116] Crop diversification was indeed a distinctive feature of Yankee farms, especially after the financial panics of the late 1830s demonstrated that concentration on a single cash crop like wheat could lead to financial disaster if the market failed.[117] Fruit trees of all kinds (apples, peaches, plums, pears, nectarines, apricots, cherries) were popular since their produce could be used for pies, preserves, and the other all-important Yankee staple, cider. Soon, too, Yankees began vegetable gardening in earnest.[118]

Both Yankees and Southerners practiced hog and cattle culture, but Yankees brought dairy farming to the Midwest (hence the wry appraisal that Yankees were "a shrewd, selfish, enterprising, cow-milking set of men").[119] At first, milk, butter, and cheese provided food for home consumption only, but once urban markets like Detroit were accessible, dairy products became an important source of cash income. Like corn liquor, butter and cheese were ideal ways a perishable product such as liquid milk could be converted into a less perishable, more portable, and more profitable form.[120] Dairy cows also brought another distinctive marker to Yankee farms: the practice of cultivating hay and other grasses for feed.[121] finally, Yankees brought sheep to Michigan as a source of wool for clothing, supplementing the flax that was used for linens.[122] Cultivating a diversity of farm products chosen for their easy marketability brought tangible material rewards in the form of considerably higher average farm incomes than for those with less diverse farms.[123]

If diversity was a hallmark of the Yankee farm, so too was openness to innovation. Many Yankees were keen to experiment with agriculture, introducing new and novel cash crops and new labor-saving devices. Our friend Lucius Lyon, for example, was one of the first to introduce the sugar beet to Michigan, hoping its sugar would become a competitive alternative to tropically grown cane sugar. Lyon also tried new varieties of melons and cabbages.[124] The fact that these early attempts usually ended in failure did not seem to daunt Lyon in the least: he was sure that if he just kept trying, he would light upon a new kind of vegetable or fruit that would make him a fortune. In addition, Yankees often looked for innovative ways to make their farms more efficient. In marked contrast to Southern farmers, who continued to use the old-style shovel plow well into the nineteenth century, Yankees quickly adopted the new cast-iron plow, which not only dug a deeper furrow but could also slice through tree roots up to four inches thick. And while Southerners clung to the use of sickles to harvest wheat, Yankees readily adopted the revolutionary mechanical grain cradle, not to mention mechanical threshers and fanning mills to accelerate harvesting.[125] Yankees literally dreamed up new and improved farm implements. In 1836, a Yankee farmer named John Hascall was worried that he could not possibly harvest all his wheat on Genesee Prairie near Schoolcraft, Michigan. One night, a radical new design for a mechanical harvester appeared to him in a dream. Confiding this to a neighbor, Hiram Moore of Comstock, who deemed the design feasible, the pair patented the harvester, enlisted investors (including, of course, Lucius Lyon), and set about building a prototype. The result was the Moore-Hascall harvesting machine, a huge contraption drawn by eight to ten teams of horses that could cover 150 acres in a season. Although the prototype was reasonably successful, Cyrus McCormack of Illinois not only created a much smaller and more wieldy machine, but he tied up Moore and Hascall's machine in a series of patent infringement suits. By the time these lawsuits were resolved, McCormack had captured the market with his admittedly superior product.[126]

The Changing Structure of the Yankee Farm Family

Throughout the colonial and antebellum periods, the structure of Yankee farm families was changing. Historians now assert that by the middle of the nineteenth century a specific "Yankee household typology" was evident in the Midwest. According to this thesis, the rise of republican and evangelical ideologies, coupled with a greater integration of capitalist markets, intensified Yankee individualism and weakened the extended family by loosening intergenerational ties. In the traditional family structure, children were expected to work well into their adult life for the good of the corporate family, and to defer whatever expectations they had for their own futures as long as their elders required. However, "Yankee families found it simpler to discard a corporate family economy and accommodate to a contractual, liberal capitalist world."[127] This had several consequences. Yankee children— even eldest sons—now saw it as their right to separate from parents at an earlier age, achieve economic independence however they could (and not necessarily by farming), and form their own nuclear families as soon as they were able. Yankee parents, in turn, began to limit the size of their families, both in order to facilitate the education of their children to face the rigors of an increasingly atomistic and competitive society, but also because large numbers of children were no longer a good "investment," since their labor would soon be lost.[128] Parents also no longer expected to live with or be supported by their children when they reached old age.[129] In fact, frequently the parents' retirement could be funded only by sale of the family farm. Yankees had long considered land as a commodity like any other, and by the late nineteenth century they had largely abandoned any sentimentality over the heirloom family farm. A farm may indeed have been passed along in the family, but by this time it was typically done through sale or lease, not by outright gift.[130]

Women bore the brunt of these changes to the Yankee farm family. With relationships weakening between women and their adult children, the conjugal tie became increasingly important to the happiness and security of farm wives. This was fine as long as harmony reigned between man and wife, but if not, women, who did not control their own wealth or property, might be forced to rely on the charity of siblings or suffer the indignity of returning to live with parents. It was perhaps for this reason that there arose throughout

The children of Francis Hodgman rake hay on a farm near Galesberg, Michigan. Hodg-man was born in 1839 in Climax Township, Michigan, to emigrant parents from New Hampshire. (Courtesy of Western Michigan University Archives and Regional History Collections.)

the Yankee Diaspora, in Michigan as well, a "nascent feminism" that advo-cated greater legal rights for women, even the possibility of divorce.[131] Even if a woman's marriage was a happy one, though, most wives could expect to outlive their husbands.[132] If well provisioned, like Melinda Nowlin, widows could live out their lives in comfort.[133] If not, they could not now automati-cally expect help from their children and might very well end up destitute.[134] Indeed, so widespread in Michigan was the plight of dispossessed Yankee widows that it became memorialized in verse. Will Carleton's "Over the Hill to the Poor-House" (1873), a plea for better treatment of farm widows, became a popular recitation piece for schoolchildren throughout the state and a spur to greater attention to this growing social problem.[135]

Yankee Community Life on the Michigan Frontier

Yankees brought with them to Michigan a strong sense of community. At first, the hardships of the frontier encouraged the kinds of informal community—known simply as "neighborliness" or "neighboring"—that had been common back in the rural districts of New England and New York. Mutual aid and informal socializing in the form of barn- and home-raisings was common, as were quilting, husking, and logging bees, and other forms of collective labor.[136] Eventually, some profit-minded Yankees would denigrate these customs as wasteful and inefficient, but during the early years in Michigan they were essential for the entire community's survival.[137]

In terms of purely recreational socializing, Yankee men and women enjoyed tea parties, card parties, fiddle dancing, storytelling (including ghost stories and war stories), and riding and sleighing. Children entertained themselves with simple games and homemade toys.[138] In addition to hunting and fishing, "base-ball" was a popular sport among pioneer Yankee boys.[139] Historian David H. Fischer, in his *Albion's Seed* (1989), reminds us that baseball, which was unknown in the South, began as "New England folk sport" and even today still "preserves a combination of order and action, reason and emotion, individuality and collective efforts which is characteristic of Puritan culture."[140] Pioneer girls, on the other hand, did not generally enjoy the same kind of freedom as boys. Destined as they were for a life of domesticity, girls' chores tended to confine them to the house.[141] It's not surprising then that the one frequent social event open to a girl—the tea party—was also a part of her domestic training.[142]

The major public holiday in the Yankee Diaspora was the Fourth of July. Independence Day celebrations were guaranteed to bring together rural communities for picnics, public oratory, and the ritual raising of the Liberty Pole.[143] Thanksgiving, of course, was the quintessential Yankee holiday, and in the early years on the frontier it was often celebrated as a community event.[144] Notably, Christmas was not a major holiday among Yankee settlers. Puritans had legally banned the celebration of Christmas as a pagan practice, and their Yankee descendents maintained the taboo as they spread west.

Excerpts from "Over the Hill to the Poor-House,"
in Will Carleton, *Farm Ballads*, 1873

Over the hill to the poor-house I'm trudgin' my weary way—
I, a woman of seventy, and only a trifle gray—
I, who am smart an' chipper, for all the years I've told,
As many another woman that's only half as old.

Over the hill to the poor-house—I can't quite make it clear!
Over the hill to the poor-house—it seems so horrid queer!
Many a step I've taken, a-toilin' to and fro,
But this is a sort of journey I never thought to go.

What is the use of heapin' on me a pauper's shame?
Am I lazy or crazy? Am I blind or lame?
True, I am not so supple, nor yet so awful stout;
But charity ain't no favor, if one can live without.

I am ready and willin' an' anxious any day
To work for a decent livin' and pay my honest way;
For I can earn my victuals, an' more too, I'll be bound,
If anybody is willin' to only have me 'round.

It was only after the Civil War, and probably in response to contacts with German and Dutch settlers who began arriving in Michigan during the 1840s, that Yankees began to observe the holiday. Yankee Yule celebrations—when they came—typically centered on the erection of a community Christmas tree in a public place such as a schoolhouse, church, or town hall. Only much later would family Christmas trees and purely private Christmas celebrations become the norm for Yankees.[145]

Formal Community

As important as informal, "neighborly" relationships were between settlers, community for Yankees was most clearly embodied in commercial

I went to live with Susan, but Susan's house was small,

And she was always a-hintin' how snug it was for us all;

And what with her husband's sisters, and what with child'rn three,

'Twas easy to discover there wasn't room for me.

An' then I went with Thomas, the oldest son I've got:

For Thomas's buildings'd cover the half of an acre lot,

But all the child'rn was on me—I couldn't stand their sauce—

And Thomas said I needn't think I was comin' there to boss.

An' then I wrote to Rebecca, my girl who lives out West,

And to Isaac, not far from her—some twenty miles at best;

And one of 'em said 'twas too warm there for anyone so old,

And t'other had an opinion the climate was too cold.

So they have shirked and slighted me, an' shifted me about—

So they have well nigh soured me, an' wore my old heart out;

But still I've borne up pretty well, an' wasn't much put down,

Till Charley went to the poor-master, an' put me on the town!

Over the hill to the poor-house—my child'rn dear, good-bye!

Many a night I've watched you when only God was nigh;

And God'll judge between us; but I will al'ays pray

That you shall never suffer the half that I do to-day!

enterprises, cultural institutions, and civil government. The earliest and most important commercial enterprises on the frontier were the gristmill and the sawmill. Such enterprises were essential for converting raw materials into finished products both for home use and, perhaps just as importantly, for cash sale on local and national markets. Mills were located wherever sufficient waterpower was available, and the most enterprising settlers competed to erect them since they often attracted the other two staple frontier enterprises, the general store and the inn with its tavern. In turn, such complexes of commercial enterprises—mill, store, and inn—often became the focal point for a rural community. If located on convenient transportation routes, such complexes had the potential to evolve into a village, town, or, for those exceptionally well placed, a city.[146] Most of the major towns and cities in southern Michigan began as places where waterpower was exceptionally good and water transportation practical; for example, Albion, Marshall, Battle Creek, Kalamazoo, and Allegan, all on the Kalamazoo River, and Grand Rapids on the Grand.[147]

As with their Puritan predecessors, for Yankees the institutions of church, school, and local government were potent symbols of social order—as necessary for a stable community as commercial enterprises.[148] No truly civilized place could be complete without them. On the frontier, however, resources were scarce and time and energy had to be devoted to mere survival. It would take years for churches and schools to develop fully in Michigan. In the meantime, Yankees improvised. Many Yankee settlers had passed some time in the "Burned-Over District" of Upstate New York and had been inspired by the revivals there.[149] To keep that spirit alive, small groups of settlers would organize themselves into interdenominational Bible study and prayer groups that met in private homes. Many Yankees would also take any opportunity to hear preaching wherever they could: for example, one of the early settlers of Gull Prairie, John Barnes, took a week out of his schedule to travel by ox cart to distant Edward's Prairie to hear a single sermon from an itinerant clergyman.[150] As mentioned previously, the major New England missionary societies were active early in sending ministers west, and Presbyterian, Congregationalist, Methodist, Baptist, and Episcopalian itinerants all vied for souls on the Michigan frontier.[151] Yankee settlers, in turn, vied to have one or more of these ministers make their settlement a regular stop on the circuit. Such impromptu religious services were held in a house, a barn, or even outdoors; then the local schoolhouse would be pressed into service; and finally a community meetinghouse would be erected. The meetinghouse was shared by all at first, at least until individual denominational groups had enough resources to construct their own buildings. Religious life on the frontier was thus ad hoc and hardly monolithic, but vibrant nonetheless. Women, especially, worked hard to create and maintain organized Christian fellowship, because of both their spiritual needs and their concern for social order, but also because this was one of the few opportunities they had to interact with other women of the neighborhood on a regular basis.[152]

Along with their focus on churches, it is hard to overestimate the importance Yankees put on schools, even on the frontier.[153] The Northwest

Ordinance of 1787 had stated that "Religion, morality, and knowledge being necessary to good government and the happiness of mankind, schools and the means of education shall forever be encouraged," a sentiment that goes back to the earliest Puritans of Massachusetts.[154] Federal legislation (1785) had already stipulated that the income on the sale or lease of section 16 of every township was to be used by territorial legislatures or state governments to support public education.[155] In this spirit, the Michigan Territorial Legislature passed in 1827 its own version of the "Old Deluder Law," obligating any township having fifty households to hire a schoolteacher.[156] However, it took time for such laws to be enforced and for funds to trickle down to the local level. In the meantime, just as Yankee settlers did not wait for the arrival of professionals to begin church groups, neither did they wait for the state to create schools. Settlers organized subscription schools or induced the township to levy a tax in order to hire a schoolmaster or mistress (typically the latter, since young women could be paid much less than men). School was first held in private homes, and then in a rough log cabin hastily constructed and furnished with puncheon benches, maybe a stove, and little else.[157] Books were scarce, all children regardless of age were taught together, and learning was done by rote with students "chant[ing] their lessons in choral form."[158] The school year lasted barely the winter months, if that. Despite these limitations, Yankees were keen that their children at least have the basic skills of reading (especially the Bible), writing, and arithmetic, since "it was a Yankee habit to equate learning with godliness, and ignorance with devilry."[159]

If the church and school were the local institutions that taught the importance of social order, the township was the local institution charged with actually maintaining it. As noted previously, the township and the town meeting were imported to Michigan from New England by way of New York. Once a critical mass of settlers had gathered in a township, they themselves would call annual elections to elect the officials that would comprise the township board. The Michigan version of the township board consisted of a supervisor, clerk, treasurer, and four justices of the peace. Additional offices included a tax assessor, a highway commissioner, a school inspector, and a sheriff or constable. The purview of the board could be wide ranging, but at the very least it was responsible for collecting taxes; disbursing poor relief; adjudicating lawsuits over debt; organizing the local school and hiring teachers; improving roads and bridges; protecting the community from crime and disturbers of the peace; and controlling animals, whether wild (e.g., bounties on wolves) or domestic.[160] For most of the nineteenth century, the township would be the level of government with which most settlers would interact on a regular basis. Township government thus took on immense importance in the life of rural Michigan communities.

Finally, once the township government was established, the church and school organized, and commercial businesses growing—in other words, once the New England social world had been replicated—Yankee settlers began to feel more at home on the Michigan frontier.

The Flowering of Yankee Michigan

This country, but a few years since, a desolate wilderness, shall like New England be spread over with churches and schoolhouses, the steady witnesses to our happiness and prosperity.

—*Detroit Courier,* September 27, 1832

By the late 1840s and 1850s, the *Detroit Courier*'s predictions were beginning to become a reality, at least in the Yankee-settled counties of southern Michigan. The worst effects of the economic depression of 1837 had faded, and many of Michigan's pioneers were feeling prosperous and secure. Log cabins were quickly being replaced with Yankee versions of Greek Revival wood-frame or brick structures, especially the ubiquitous "upright-and-wing" houses so popular with Yankees from Upstate New York.[161] And despite the fact that a raft of state-sponsored internal improvements, including canals and railroads, had fallen victim to the economic downturn, roads had improved and communications with the East were faster. Farm products were easier to send to more distant markets, and a greater variety of eastern manufactured goods began to appear in the local general store. The mails moved faster, with news arriving within days of an event, not weeks.

The pioneer's sense of isolation was passing away. Michigan was moving beyond the frontier stage.

The Growth of Yankee Towns

Perhaps nothing better exemplifies the passing of the frontier era than the rise of the Yankee town in Michigan. Many Yankees craved town life, and with good reason. Their Puritan ancestors had come largely from villages and towns in England and had sought to recreate this urban life in New England. Towns, for Puritans, came to represent the ideal social order, offering tight-knit community, opportunities for education, and, above all, a disciplined religious life.[162] For economic reasons having to do with the availability of land, their descendents often sacrificed this Puritan ideal for material gain, but many Yankees never lost their taste for town life. Indeed, in the Midwest, Yankee farmers were far more likely than their non-Yankee neighbors to sell or lease their farms and move to town, especially if they felt it would be more profitable.[163] For those who did not abandon farming, the Yankee desire to be close to town created a situation in which prosperous Yankee farmers tended to monopolize the land closest to town, inflating land values around urban areas and relegating less prosperous non-Yankees to a distant periphery. As historian Daniel Campbell found in the case of Marshall, Michigan, this, in turn, tended to create a relatively homogeneous Yankee farm belt around a town, thus intensifying Yankee influence over a town's development.[164] This is not to say, of course, that the towns themselves were culturally homogeneous; this was never the case. However, given the Yankee predilection for town life, and given the strength of Yankee migration during this period, most towns in Michigan took on a distinctly Yankee flavor.

Not surprisingly, Yankees in Michigan modeled their towns' development after towns they had known in Upstate New York and New England. These eastern towns had undergone significant changes during the first decades of the nineteenth century, and Michigan towns reflected these changes. For one thing, as the commercial economy expanded, production and retail moved out of the home and into specialized districts. Thus, instead of the traditional town that grew organically without planning, towns in the northeast and Up-state New York came to be platted on a grid with commercial areas separated from residential neighborhoods. As Michigan's commercial crossroads, with their single street and mix of businesses and dwellings, grew into full-fledged towns, they too became differentiated: domestic districts were soon segregated from retail and manufacturing districts, and all contained within a grid of parallel streets and rectangular lots.[165] The reason for this differentiation goes back to the perennial tension in Yankee culture between the demands of the market and the demands of community. Wishing to participate freely in the market, yet realizing its potential corrosiveness to communal values, Yankees sought to insulate the institutions of social order—family, church, school, and to a lesser degree, government—by physically separating them from the market. As economic life intensified in the antebellum period, so too did the drive for concerted urban planning.

The desire to protect communal life from the rapacity of economic life not only impacted the structure of Yankee towns, but that of Yankee families as well. In those families who could afford it—the emerging middle class— mothers stayed at home with children, while fathers worked outside the home, usually in another district of town off limits to women and children.[166] Ideally, fathers were to be the principal breadwinner of the family, skilled at negotiating in the often-unscrupulous business world. Mothers' principal responsibility, meanwhile, was maintenance of the household and, most importantly, childcare. This last contributed to a major shift in the way children were raised. Where in traditional families fathers ruled their children through fear and unquestioning discipline, mothers "sought to develop the children's conscience and their capacity to love, to teach them to make good moral choices, and to prepare themselves for conversion and a lifetime of Christian service."[167] Women, therefore, came to be the moral center of this new type of family structure, thus leading to the feminization of family life that historians have labeled the "cult of domesticity."[168] In the "new domestic order," men were expected to respect the boundaries between their public life in the world and the intensely private life of home. As one wag put it, this created a "Half-Male, Half-Female culture in which the man spelled 'pray' with an *a* at home and with an *e* at the office."[169] The importance of this development can hardly be overestimated: in time, the new Yankee family structure would become "the foundation for the American middle-class." Of course, not all Yankee families at the time embraced these changes, either because they could not afford them or because of a strong streak of cultural conservatism, or both. As a result, Michigan's Yankee towns during this period came to exhibit greater class distinctions between "Big Yankees" and "Little Yankees," that is, between those families who benefited financially from the new market economy and who embraced the new middle-class ethos, and those who didn't.[170] Such class divisions would be endemic in Michigan and the rest of the Yankee Diaspora throughout the nineteenth century.

The Expansion of Education

The evolution of middle-class family life not only changed the roles of fathers and mothers, but of children as well. Middle-class families now put less emphasis on child labor and more emphasis on child nurture. Childhood would now be a time for preparation for the future, and children, as much as possible, would now be shielded from the harsh realties of life until they reached maturity. For example, the practice of apprenticeship for boys had almost disappeared by 1850.[171] Education, therefore, came to be the focus of childhood. As we have seen, rudimentary education had long been valued in Yankee communities, but as Yankee towns developed, educational opportunities expanded correspondingly. In addition to the tax-supported public school, towns now offered a variety of private academies devoted to classical studies or female education, as well as Sabbath schools devoted to basic religious and civic instruction. Several of these private schools were taught by Yankee ministers hoping to improve their incomes, and most were short-lived.[172] However, they did indicate a growing desire for higher education, and this in turn would fuel the expansion of Michigan's public school system beyond the one-room schoolhouse.

Two Yankees, Isaac Crary and the Reverend John Pierce, both early settlers of Marshall, are credited with laying the groundwork for Michigan's comprehensive public school system—the first in the nation. Ever since the founding of the Republic, a fierce debate had been raging over the desirability of a centrally coordinated and state-funded system of public education.[173] New Englanders tended to favor state support (as witnessed by the state funding written into the Land Ordinance of 1785), but centralization was still controversial. Crary, a lawyer, and Pierce, a Congregationalist minister and headmaster, impressed by reports of the successes of the Prussian school system, felt that the time was ripe for such a coordinated state system, and they worked tirelessly to promote it. Crary was appointed to chair the Committee on Public Education at the Michigan Constitutional Convention of 1835, where he proposed three constitutional measures: the creation of the office of state superintendent of schools; state supervision of educational funds generated by the sale of federal lands; and the establishment of an endowment for the University of Michigan.[174] These were accepted and duly ratified, and John Pierce was appointed the first superintendent of public instruction. Pierce, in turn, proposed that the state create an ambitious system of branch academies to function as teacher training schools and as conduits for students to the University of Michigan. Branches were indeed established at Pontiac, Monroe, Kalamazoo, Detroit, Niles, White Pigeon, Tecumseh, and Romeo, although all were closed within a few years. Despite this, the foundation had been laid for the interlocking system of primary and secondary schools, normal schools, and state universities that would develop later in the century.[175]

Not all education in towns was formal education. Newspapers became far more widespread, with even small towns supporting more than one newssheet, usually representing differing political allegiances. Supplies of books and magazines, primarily printed in New England, were now more available and affordable.[176] Yankees brought with them to Michigan a propensity to form voluntary organizations to promote literary and other intellectual pursuits among adults. As early as 1818, the Detroit Ladies Society was formed under the sponsorship of Yankee-Yorker Augustus Woodward (one of the founders of the "Catholepistemiad," forerunner of the University of Michigan). The same year saw the founding of the Detroit Mechanic's Society, followed by the Detroit Reading Club (1825), Detroit City Library (1817), Detroit Athenaeum (1831), and Young Men Society (1833), a reading club for clerks. Few of Michigan's small towns could match Detroit's diversity of such enterprises, but few wholly lacked some form of debating society, reading club, or lending library. The Lyceum circuit, which had originated with Joseph Holbrook of Massachusetts in 1826, brought itinerant lecturers on a variety of topics to Michigan's towns beginning in the 1830s; later in the century, the Lyceum would be superseded by another Yankee educational invention, the summer Chautauqua.[177]

A particularly noteworthy development during this period was the increasing participation of women in the creation of these extramural educational institutions. Now that they took a greater hand in the education of their children, middle-class mothers sought greater access to education for themselves. For example, the Ladies' Library Association of Kalamazoo, called an "outpost of New England culture," was the first all-female organization to be chartered in Michigan (1852). According to its constitution, the association was for the "encouragement and maintenance of a library, to afford and encourage useful and entertaining reading; to furnish literary and scientific lectures; and other means of promoting moral and intellectual improvement in the town of Kalamazoo."[178] The Ladies' Library Association of Kalamazoo continues in operation to this day.

Yankee Religion in Michigan

Religion continued to be as important to town Yankees as it was in the rural countryside, but with two major differences. First, a higher percentage of urban dwellers actually formally affiliated with a church, both because it was more convenient to do so and because social pressure was stronger in town (in the countryside, only about 15 to 20 percent were formal members of a congregation).[179] The second major difference was that towns offered more religious choices than were possible in the countryside. As a result, full-blown denominationalism asserted itself. By and large, denominational divisions reflected class differences between "Big Yankees" and "Little Yankees." Congregationalism, Presbyterianism, and Episcopalianism tended to attract middle and upper class Yankees.[180] All three—classified by historians as "formalist" churches—stressed a highly intellectualized faith, an educated clergy, and fairly elaborate liturgies. Each, at one time, had been an established or state-supported church, and thus their ministers still felt that they had the right to community leadership. Formalists were highly optimistic about the reformation of society at large and were at home in the secular world. The Methodists and Baptists, on the other hand, recruited largely from the lower classes. Their faith was simple, their clergy less polished, and their services plain but infused with high emotion. These "antiformalists" were also less sanguine about the perfectibility of society; their goal was first and foremost the salvation of individual souls, and while they enthusiastically participated in the great moral crusades of the day, they tended to retain their sectarian character and maintain a certain cautiousness toward the secular world. Not surprisingly, one of the major differences between formalists and antiformalists was in their attitudes toward the growth of market society: whereas the formalists were apt to identify economic development as "the march of progress," antiformalists, not so successful in the market society, preserved the old Puritan wariness toward moneymaking, fearing that the new economic order was "a descent into worldliness that would almost certainly provoke God's wrath."[181] Gradually, Yankee Methodists and Baptists in Michigan would assimilate to a more pro-market position, become more prosperous, and eventually become more formalistic, but these transitions would occur only much later in the century. Until that time, class remained a salient feature of Yankee religion in Michigan.

Despite their differences, four of these five denominations (Methodist, Baptist, Congregationalist, and Presbyterian) can be classified together as evangelical—that is, they felt strongly that their mission included conversion of the unchurched through aggressive missionary outreach. All four evangelical traditions carried into Michigan memories of the religious fervor of the Burned-Over District and the Second Great Awakening. Throughout the antebellum period, periodic small-scale revivals were common in the Yankee portions of the state. Methodists brought to Michigan the outdoor camp meeting, which had been so wildly successful on the frontier in Kentucky and other western states. In time, these camp meetings were institutionalized into permanent summer camps, the most famous of which was the Tony Bay View Assembly on the shores of Little Traverse Bay near Petoskey.[182]

All four evangelical denominations also took to heart Lyman Beecher's injunction to evangelize the West through higher education. Despite an early state law that made it difficult to charter denominational colleges, which were feared as competitors with the infant University of Michigan, evangelical ministers persisted and eventually prevailed. The first was Thomas Merrill, a Baptist missionary from Maine, who managed to secure a charter in 1833 for the Michigan and Huron Institute, later Kalamazoo College. The Methodists followed with Albion College (1839), the Presbyterians with Marshall College (1839), and the Congregationalists with Olivet College (1844). This last was the brainchild of the Reverend J. J. Shipherd, co-founder of that quintessential Midwestern Yankee college, Oberlin, in Ohio. Reflecting Oberlin's radicalism, Olivet was the first college in the nation to admit both women and African Americans from the first opening of

The Congregationalist Revolt in Michigan

Given the preponderance of Yankees in Michigan, it might be expected that the state would have been a stronghold of Congregationalism from the start. This was not the case. During the eighteenth century, Methodists and Baptists had drawn a significant number of Yankees away from Congregationalism, and in Michigan, Methodist circuit riders and Baptist farmer-preachers had stolen a march on the old Puritan church. Indeed, even Presbyterianism was better represented during Michigan's pioneer days, due to a missionary arrangement called the "Plan of Union." Recognizing their doctrinal closeness, and not wishing to compete with one another, New England Congregationalists agreed in 1801 to cooperate with the Scotch-Irish-dominated Presbyterian General Assembly in evangelizing the West. Congregationalist and Presbyterian settlers on the frontier were encouraged to form themselves into one "Presbygational" congregation, with issues of polity (congregational independence vs. top-down control by a presbytery) decided by a majority vote. Soon, though, it was clear that the Presbyterians were gaining the upper hand in the arrangement, since they enjoyed a more robust national organization. Among many Yankee settlers this was a dismaying development, since the sacrifice of Congregationalism would signal the loss of a significant aspect of their Yankee identity. Isaac W. Ruggles, the first

its doors. Even smaller denominations representing Yankee-led schisms from the evangelical "big four" also founded colleges in Michigan: for example, the Freewill Baptists founded Michigan Central College (1844), later Hillsdale College, and the Wesleyan Methodists, Adrian College (1859). Of these antebellum Yankee colleges, only Marshall College did not survive (although the Presbyterians also supported Olivet and founded the still operating Alma College in the 1880s). Considering this rate of success, the educational legacy of antebellum Yankee evangelicals has had a formidable and lasting impact on the state.[183]

New Yankee Religions in Michigan

Yankee religious diversity went beyond the five major denominations mentioned so far. As Yankees poured into Michigan, this diversity manifested

Congregationalist minister in Michigan, steadfastly refused to be a party to the Plan of Union. From his arrival in 1824, Ruggles itinerated through the Yankee settlements of Oakland and Macomb counties, founding a number of specifically Congregationalist churches (Sweet 1964, 29–34). Ruggles was joined in 1831 by John D. Pierce, a minister who, in his own words, refused to abandon the "Congregational faith and polity of the Pilgrim Fathers of Plymouth Rock." When told that he should found only Presbyterian congregations because, "while Congregationalism did well enough for New England, it was not adapted to the recent settlements of the west," Pierce replied, "if [Congregationalism] was adapted to . . . New England in its infancy, it would not be less so to the new settlements of the west" (Pierce 1881, 351, 354). Pierce, like Ruggles, rejected the Plan and went on to organize several Congregationalist churches in and around Marshall. In time, enough like-mined ministers and congregations were formed that they confederated into the Michigan General Association in 1842, and when the Plan of Union finally dissolved in 1852 in response to resurgent Congregationalism in New England, the denomination in Michigan entered a period of sustained growth, from 53 churches in 1845 to 269 churches in 1885 (Sweet 1964, 33; Hurd 1886, 109; for a detailed history of the breakup of the Plan of Union in Michigan, see Kuhns 1948, 157–80).

itself, with congregations of Yankee Universalists, Unitarians, Swedenborgians, and Spiritualists finding homes in the growing towns of southern Michigan. Of these smaller religious groups, perhaps the most colorful were the Strangite Mormons and the Seventh-Day Adventists. Both were new Yankee religions with roots in the Burned-Over District of Upstate New York and the Second Great Awakening. Mormonism, officially known as the Church of Jesus Christ of Latter-day Saints, was founded by Vermont-born Joseph Smith in 1830.[184] Based in part on a set of newly revealed scriptures, *The Book of Mormon,* this new sect reiterated a number of old Puritan themes: Mormons were God's chosen people, whose task it was to purify the Church of Christ and establish an American Bible commonwealth in anticipation of the Second Coming. Mormonism spread quickly among the Yankees of the Midwest, with sizeable communities forming in northern Ohio, Missouri, and Illinois. As early as 1831, Mormon missionaries were successfully proselytizing in Pontiac, Michigan.[185] Because of their treatment of outsiders, and because of some of their distinctive practices—not least of which was polygamy—the Mormons were not well liked by their neighbors and encountered escalating persecution and violence. Joseph Smith was murdered by a mob in 1844, and three years later, in an effort to find a safe haven, the majority of Mormons migrated to the Great Salt Lake under the leadership of another Vermonter, Brigham Young.

Not all Mormons headed west, though. Some elected to follow James Jesse Strang, a Yankee-Yorker who claimed to be the rightful heir to Smith.[186] Strang established a community at Voree, Wisconsin, but fearing persecution, he moved his group to Beaver Island in northern Lake Michigan in 1847. Once established on the island, Strang had himself crowned king and regent of God, instituted polygamy, laid down a strict set of "Mosaic" laws for life in his kingdom, and gradually ousted non-Mormons from the island. Strang also managed to dominate county government and was twice elected to the Michigan State Legislature. Alas, Strang's vision of an island kingdom was short-lived: in 1856, the "King" was assassinated by two disgruntled members and the Beaver Island Strangites fell victim to the depredations of the Irish fishermen whom they had so ruthlessly displaced. Within a few years, little remained of the "Kingdom of St. James."

More successful and having a greater lasting impact on Michigan were the Seventh-Day Adventists.[187] Adventism is derived from the teachings of William Miller, a Baptist farmer-preacher from Upstate New York who, based on numerical clues in the Bible, calculated that Jesus was destined to return in 1844. For a time, Miller attracted a fair number of followers, but when his predictions failed to come true, most "Millerites" abandoned the prophet and returned to their old denominations. A few hardy souls persevered, including Ellen Harmon from Maine. Harmon was a seer in her own right and was subject to visions that tended to confirm Miller's conviction that Christ's Second Advent was imminent. She also taught that to merit Christ's kingdom, believers had to, among other things, strive to live a healthy lifestyle and celebrate the Sabbath on Saturday—hence "Seventh-day" Adventism. In 1846, Harmon married the Adventist preacher and publisher James White, and together they traveled New England on preaching tours before settling in Rochester, New York, in 1852. James White set to work editing the *Advent Review and Sabbath Herald* and Ellen White began her own remarkable writing career, eventually producing some fifty books and countless articles promoting the Adventist cause.

The Adventists' connection to Michigan began in 1855 when a sympathetic businessman from Battle Creek offered the Whites the use of his publishing house. Sensing that the future of Adventism lay in the West, the Whites relocated, and for decades to come this small Michigan town would be the headquarters for this growing religious movement. It was here that the Seventh-day Adventists organized themselves into a legally recognized denomination and built the substantial brick church known as the Dime Tabernacle (so-called because it was funded in part by the donations of Adventist children). It was here, too, that Ellen White developed her theology of health reforms, which included abstention from alcohol, caffeinated drinks, excess sugar, and, if possible, meat. She also promoted dress reform for women, advocating the use of the "Bloomer costume," and a variety of physical therapies then popular, especially hydropathy, or the "water cure." In order to provide the benefits of the water-cure regimen to her followers, Ellen White opened the Western Health Reform Institute in Battle Creek in 1866. The Institute eventually became the Battle Creek Sanitarium, or simply "the San," and under the leadership of Dr. John Harvey Kellogg it was destined to become one of the premiere health resorts of the nineteenth century and the birthplace of Kellogg's Cornflakes. "The San" was simply the first in a string of such therapeutic institutions, including hospitals and medical colleges, sponsored by the Seventh-day Adventist Church. In addition to her prophetic and health concerns, Ellen White also shared the common Yankee concern for education. She envisioned schools that wove the Adventist message into a largely vocational program such that children would be fitted to live a committed Christian life in a rapidly changing, ruthlessly competitive society. To this end, White created the Battle Creek College in 1874 to serve as the capstone for a series of private Adventist primary and secondary schools around the nation.

Despite her forward-looking reformism, Ellen White's educational ideas reflect the fact that she always remained a "Little Yankee" at heart. After the Civil War, White looked with alarm at the effects of rapid industrialization and the spread of unbridled market capitalism. With the death of her husband in 1881, White increasingly spent time in rural California and later abroad, including a decade doing mission work in Australia. She returned to Battle

Creek in 1900, but she was repelled by the commercial culture of the town, which, ironically, her Health Institute had indirectly fueled. She moved the College, later renamed Andrews University, to Berrien Springs, and, when the Adventist Publishing House burned in 1901, White took this opportunity to move the headquarters for Seventh-day Adventism to Takoma Park, outside of Washington, D.C. White herself retreated to St. Helena, California, where she died in 1915. By this time, Seventh-day Adventism had grown to be a well-established denomination of international scope.

Yankee Social Reform

While they may have differed in theologies, one issue that did unite all Yankee evangelicals in Michigan was a continuing devotion to social reform. Not all evangelicals agreed on which aspects of society were in most need of reform, but all agreed that reformation was essential, particularly in light of the vertiginous social changes catalyzed by the new market economy and urbanization. Three reform movements were especially popular among Michigan's Yankees: Sabbatarianism, temperance, and abolitionism. Puritans and their heirs had long been keen to observe the Fourth Commandment, and legislating a strict Sabbatarianism was second nature to these communities. We have already seen this in the case of Vermontville, but it should be mentioned that as early as 1820, the territorial government passed a statute prohibiting on Sunday the "exercise of any secular labor, business or employment, except such as necessary and acts of charity shall require." It also prohibited the "exercise or use of any games, sports or plays, or hold or resort to any public assembly, except such as shall be holden for the purpose of social and religious worship and moral instruction."[188] As the century progressed, the need to protect the Sabbath became even more urgent. In order to be competitive, more businesses found it necessary to be open on Sundays, and the introduction of the railroads meant that many a small town's Sabbath would be disrupted by the noisy passage of trains. Eventually, the state legislature banned Sunday train service (except when it involved the U.S. mails), although this was soon relaxed to allow at least one passenger train on that day.[189] The development and diversification of towns also brought new sources of amusement, such as theaters and circuses, which competed with churches for an audience, as did the phenomenon of

Sunday baseball. Several towns passed local ordinances against such activities, which they then proceeded to rigorously enforce. An 1867 edition of the *Detroit Free Press,* for example, reported that a group of boys were arrested and spent a night in jail for the crime of playing baseball on the Sabbath.[190]

Yankee Sabbatarianism in Michigan was often bound up with the promotion of temperance. Throughout the antebellum period, Americans routinely imbibed a prodigious amount of alcohol; historians estimate that the average male consumed the equivalent of 7.1 gallons of pure alcohol annually.[191] In addition to casual consumption, the custom of "neighboring," from husking bees to barn raisings, typically involved copious amounts of corn liquor to relieve the tediousness of the work. Such drinking inevitably led to high rates of alcoholism, spousal abuse, desertion of children, and a whole host of other social evils. Beginning with the Second Great Awakening, therefore, evangelical Yankees such as Kalamazoo's Augustus Littlejohn sought to solve the nation's drinking problem either by limiting it to beer or wine (temperance) or by forgoing alcohol altogether (complete abstinence or "teetotalism").[192]

The inflow of Irish and Germans during this period only exacerbated the alcohol problem, and, in the eyes of the Yankees, it did so in a particularly egregious way: these largely Catholic immigrants practiced what was disparagingly called the "Continental Sabbath"—that is, church in the morning and socializing, including social drinking, in the afternoon. In order to curtail the latter activity, Michigan Yankees, beginning in the 1820s, sought to legislate limits on Sunday liquor sales. Most of these laws were hard to enforce and were widely flouted; by mid-century, Detroit alone, a city of only forty-five thousand people, had more than five hundred saloons, bars, and grog shops. Nevertheless, evangelical Yankees persisted, for, as Lyman Beecher had told the Detroit Temperance Society, "The millennium could never come while such an evil was in the world."[193] Inspired by the passage of the 1852 Maine Law, which prohibited the manufacture and sale of any alcoholic beverage in that New England state, Michigan Yankees rushed to propose a similar law, which was duly passed by the legislature and approved by the majority of voters in a referendum in 1853. This law (called by the Detroit *Catholic Vindicator* "a tyrannical puritan blue law") was declared unconstitutional by the courts, so the legislature tried again in 1855.[194] This prohibition law passed judicial muster, but as with the local option and Sunday closing laws, prohibition was impossible to enforce and was repealed in 1875.[195] Despite these defeats, Michigan's evangelical Yankees persevered, keeping the twin dreams of temperance and strict Sabbatarianism alive well into the twentieth century.

Abolitionism in Michigan

Abolition of slavery in the United States was the third great social reform movement that excited Michigan's Yankees. The first anti-slavery society in Michigan was founded in Adrian in 1832, followed by the founding of the Detroit Antislavery Society in 1834 and eighteen more such societies throughout the state within four years.[196] Yankee abolitionists were drawn primarily from the evangelical churches, and of these, the most militant were the Baptists, Congregationalists, and Methodists. As early as 1840, the Michigan Baptist Convention passed a resolution stating, "That the sin of slavery will remain in all its hated forms in these United States until the professors of our holy religion take a decided stand against this evil, demoralizing to the slaveholder and destructive to the soul and body of the slave, and thus clear their skirts of the most cursed evil of the land." As long as Congregationalists were submerged in the Plan of Union, abolitionist sentiments were muted, since the Presbyterian Church was a national church with many members in the South. However, the moment the Congregationalists broke away, the Michigan General Association became increasingly vociferous in their demands for the "speedy and utter extermination of this complicated evil from the land."[197] Michigan's Methodists, too, belonged to a national organization with a sizable southern membership that sought to quash debate over slavery. Frustrated by this gag rule, a number of Michigan's Yankee Methodists broke away from the Methodist Episcopal Church to form the Wesleyan Methodist Church of Michigan in 1841; two years later, inspired by this bold move, a convention met in Utica, New York, to unite like-minded Methodists into the Wesleyan Methodist Connection of America. By the 1850s, Michigan's Methodist Episcopal Conference had also broken away from the national organization over the same issue.[198]

Although strongly anti-slavery in sentiment, Yankee attitudes toward African Americans themselves were, like those of most white Americans of the time, complex. Most who favored slavery's abolition hardly favored social equality for blacks. John Ball, seemingly one of the more thoughtful and humane Yankees ever to settle in Michigan, held little hope that blacks and whites could coexist. After passing a winter in Darien, Georgia, in 1821, he wrote, "Saw much that satisfied me that the African and the Caucasian are constitutionally unlike, and cannot by any education be made, even to fully understand each other, any more than the ox and the horse. Each may have good qualities, but each in his own way."[199] Flavius Littlejohn (brother of Augustus) went further, for while he was an abolitionist, he feared racial "amalgamation" and was dead set against giving freed blacks the vote, a position seconded by John Pierce, the "father of Michigan schools."[200] Indeed, while the 1827 Michigan territorial legislature passed a law giving freed blacks protection from Southern slave raiders, it expressly denied them state citizenship and discouraged them from migrating to the state. The first Michigan Constitutional Convention acted the same: slavery was banned in the state, but, after vigorous debate, black suffrage was not approved. Blacks would not receive the vote in Michigan until 1870.[201]

For those Yankee abolitionists whose racism precluded social equality for blacks, their hatred of the "peculiar institution" had more to do with what they perceived as the unfair political and economic advantages slavery gave to the South, and the negative impact the expansion of slavery would have on free soil and free labor. As one minister from Ohio put it, "They had no pity for the black man enslaved but when the Slave Lord sought to gag and manacle the Yankees that altered the case." If this were to change, the South needed to be subdued and that could be achieved only through the abolition of black slavery. What happened to the freed slaves after that would then be the South's problem. A few Yankee abolitionists, however, believed that granting equal rights for blacks was the logical corollary to abolitionism and cared deeply for the fate of freed blacks. Austin Blair, who would eventually be elected governor of Michigan, wrote an impassioned plea for black suffrage while serving in the state legislature in 1846. In it, Blair pointed out that "He who may not vote is as powerless practically as if he were dead or enslaved." Moreover, in those Michigan towns where Yankee evangelicalism flourished, both abolitionism *and* black suffrage were likely to have strong support.[202]

Of all Michigan's religious groups, it was the Quakers who did the most practical good for the state's small black population. Repelled by slavery and by harsh laws regulating the lives of freed slaves, southern Quakers often migrated to the Northwest in company with freed blacks from their home neighborhoods. Wherever there were Quaker settlements in Michigan, such as in Cass County, there also black families could be found. Most Quakers were born in the South or the Middle States, but one of Michigan's most famous Quakers—Laura Smith Haviland—was a representative of the Yankee strain of Quakerism.[203] Born in 1808 to a Yankee-Yorker father and a Vermonter mother, Haviland spent her childhood in Upstate New York, where she attended a Quaker school. In 1825, she married a Quaker farmer named Charles Haviland Jr. and the couple moved to a Quaker settlement in Raisin Township in Lenawee County, Michigan. The Havilands were well matched: both had imbibed the Burned-Over District's evangelical spirit and both shared the humanitarian concerns of the Benevolent Empire. Education was one their chief concerns. In 1837, they began a school for orphans and impoverished children that in time evolved into the Raisin Institute, a manual labor school patterned after Oberlin and admitting all regardless of sex or color. Abolitionism, of course, was a central concern. Upon moving to Raisin Township, the Havilands met the ardent Quaker abolitionist Elizabeth M. Chandler, and together they formed what was reputed to be the first antislavery society in Michigan. Not all of their Quaker neighbors approved of such "ultraist" activity, however. In protest, the Havilands broke with the Quakers and joined the more congenial Wesleyan Methodist Church, in which denomination Laura Haviland would become an ordained minister (she would eventually reunite with the Quakers in 1872).

After an 1845 epidemic took her husband and much of her family, Laura Haviland launched herself into a whirlwind of antislavery activities, all of which was strenuous and much of it dangerous. From then until the outbreak of the Civil War, Haviland conducted missionary work among freed slaves in both the Northwest and the South; traveled widely in the Midwest and Canada, helping to coordinate the Underground Railroad; and, in a time when women rarely spoke in public, she became an accomplished and sought-after abolitionist speaker who was so fearless that she even preached her antislavery message in Kentucky and Arkansas. During the Civil War, Haviland visited soldiers in Army hospitals and advocated for the relief of refugee slaves and their children; after the war, she gained an appointment to the Michigan Freedmen's Aid Commission, and in that capacity she worked tirelessly to ameliorate the conditions of freed slaves in the southern states and Kansas. Eventually, Haviland would return to Michigan, where

Laura S. Haviland. (Frontispiece from Laura S. Haviland, Woman's Life-Work: Including Thirty Years' Service on the Underground Railroad and in the War *[Grand Rapids, Mich.: S. B. Shaw, 1881].)*

she continued to work for the welfare of African Americans. She would also renew her interest in education for the disadvantaged, and, true to her Yankee roots, take up new causes such as temperance and women's suffrage. Before her death in Grand Rapids at the ripe old age of eighty-nine, Laura Haviland had even become a bestselling author with her autobiography, *A Woman's Life-Work* (1881), a remarkable and sometimes thrilling portrait of her life as an abolitionist and crusader for the rights of African Americans.

Michigan Yankees, the Rise of the Republican Party, and the Civil War

The rise of towns in Michigan paralleled the intensification of partisan politics in the state. The two major political parties during the antebellum period were the Democrats and the Whigs. In many ways, the split between these two parties mirrored the larger tensions in Yankee society. As the historian Martin Hershock put it, "Those individuals who embraced the modern world market . . . tended to become Whigs. By contrast, those who believed that modernity had unleashed an impersonal and aggressive, predatory tide upon innocent Americans . . . chose instead to join the ranks of the Democratic Party."[204] Another crucial difference between the parties was that the Whigs maintained the old Puritan concern for controlling personal morality, whereas the Democrats embodied a more liberal attitude toward individual behavior. In sum, the Whig vision of American society was more communalistic and hierarchical, while the Democratic vision was more individualistic and egalitarian. Significantly, during Michigan's territorial period, the Democrats had a stronger and more disciplined national party organization, which allowed Democrats to dominate Michigan's politics for decades. Lewis Cass and Lucius Lyon, for example, were both dyed-in-the-wool Democrats. On the other hand, a substantial portion of the Yankee population of Michigan—especially those "Big Yankees" with evangelical leanings—were diehard Whigs. Beginning with the 1840 presidential campaign, in which Yankee cultural symbols were made good use of to get out the vote for William Henry Harrison, Michigan's Whigs became better organized and more competitive.[205] Yet, while both parties had their share of Yankee antislavery men, the Whigs tended to have a greater percentage of "ultraist" abolitionists, and these people tended to get siphoned off into the Liberty Party and later the Free Soil Party, thus undermining Whig chances for electoral success. Until the rise of the Republican Party, Michigan was squarely a Democratic state.

Michigan is one of at least three states that claim to be the birthplace of the Republican Party, although Michigan's claim is strong.[206] Incensed by the passage of the Kansas-Nebraska Act in 1854, many northerners sought ways to unify antislavery, anti-southern sentiment under the banner of one "fusion" party. "Anti-Nebraska" conventions designed for this purpose met in Wisconsin, Washington, D.C., Maine, and New York, but the new party really coalesced only at an antislavery convention on July 6, 1854, in Jackson, Michigan. Over three thousand people responded to the call, thus necessitating an outdoor meeting. Here, "under the oaks," Whigs, Democrats, Free Soilers, and others abandoned their previous party loyalties and pledged to create the Republican Party. The extent to which this was a party of Yankee unity cannot be overestimated, and it was precisely because of the state's preponderance of Yankees that the necessary momentum for the formation of a new political party was found specifically in Michigan. It is estimated that 70 percent of all Republicans in Michigan were Yankees, making it "more homogeneously Yankee in spirit and membership than the Whigs had been."[207] Most of the early support for the Republicans in Michigan came from the south central counties settled primarily by Yankees; these counties routinely gave Republican candidates 60 to 75 percent of the vote.[208] One of the first such candidates was Kingsley S. Bingham, an ex-Democrat Yankee-Yorker elected to the governorship in 1855. Kingsley's election signaled the beginning of Republican dominance of state politics that would last well into the next century. Of course, the founding of the Republican Party in Michigan would have more transcendental effects: very quickly the party would gain a strong following throughout the North, and its electoral victories—especially that of Abraham Lincoln—would soon precipitate the Civil War.

When the war came in 1861, Michigan's Yankees participated enthusiastically, making the state one of the strongest supporters of the war effort. Thousands of Michigan's Yankees and Yankee-Yorkers flocked to enlist, abandoning farms, businesses, and families to take part in what many thought at first would be a great adventure and an easy victory. Some would find glory, like Armada's Private John A. Huff, killer of J. E. B. Stuart, or Allegan's Colonel Benjamin J. Pritchard, capturer of Jefferson Davis.[209] Most would fight anonymously, suffer in silence, and return profoundly changed by the searing experience of the world's first "total war."

For many Michiganders, the Civil War was the inevitable, if regrettable, final step in the crusade to extend Yankee culture in the face of a recalcitrant and treasonous South. Politically, the old compromisers like Lewis Cass stepped aside as a new generation of radicalized Michigan Yankees such as Austin Blair and Zachariah Chandler took charge. Blair, a product of the Burned-Over District and a staunch abolitionist living in Jackson, was one of the founders of the Republican Party. While he initially supported his fellow Yankee-Yorker, William Seward, for the 1860 Republican presidential nomination, he threw his support behind the eventual nominee, Abraham Lincoln, and found himself swept into the governorship with Lincoln's election. In his inaugural address, Blair declared that the Union must be preserved at all costs, and that "secession is revolution and revolution is the overt act of treason and must be treated as such."[210] Thus, when the War Department requested troops from Michigan, Blair personally raised $81,020 to create the First Michigan Infantry. Michigan's was the first regiment from the western states to arrive in Washington, D.C., reportedly prompting Lincoln's relieved exclamation, "Thank God for Michigan!"[211] Throughout the war, Blair maintained his steadfast support for the Union cause, although, until the Emancipation Proclamation, the governor criticized President Lincoln for not explicitly making the war into a crusade to abolish slavery.[212]

Even more truculent in this regard was New Hampshire–born Zachariah Chandler, elected Republican senator from Michigan in 1857, serving (with a hiatus) until 1879.[213] A successful businessman and prominent abolitionist whose Detroit home was a stop on the Underground Railroad, Chandler welcomed the war, stating famously in a letter to Blair that "without a little blood-letting this Union will not, in my estimation, be worth a rush."[214] In the U.S. Senate, Chandler was leader of the radical Republicans who pushed for the most ruthless prosecution of the war. After the fall of Confederacy, "Michigan's fire-eater" was in the forefront of the Radical Reconstruction movement and championed the passage of the Thirteenth, Fourteenth, and Fifteenth Amendments to the United States Constitution (this despite the fact that Michigan itself would not allow black suffrage for several more years). Well into the 1870s, Chandler would continue to pound away at anyone who counseled lenience toward the South. Eventually, Blair's and Chandler's radicalism fell out of step with the cooling temper of the nation. As historian Robert Kelly put it, "For most Americans, the Civil War had drained away the spirit that had inspired abolitionism and the holy Yankee crusade against Southernism. The conflict's enormity simply had left them exhausted."[215] With the South conquered and slavery abolished, many of Michigan's Yankees had grown weary of Southern issues at the termination of the War. Many Yankees had already turned their considerable energies to another holy crusade: making money.

The Industrialization of Yankee Michigan

[T]he New England banker, railroad promoter, merchant, and manufacturer, also lifted his eyes to a farther horizon and followed with his vision the extending frontier of New England's western sons. . . . [New England] tended to follow the trail of her pioneers to new industrial empires.

—Frederick Jackson Turner, "Greater New England in
the Middle of the Nineteenth Century," 1919

The Civil War stimulated Michigan's economic growth, catalyzing its transformation from an agricultural to an industrial economy.[216] During the war, extractive industries in Michigan such as mining and logging grew by leaps and bounds, and manufacturing exploded. Acute labor shortages caused by the war created markets for new labor-saving machines and more efficient production processes. Moreover, the war closed the Mississippi River, the major route to national and international markets for much Midwest grain. To take advantage of this, Michigan provided greater outlets to the East by investing in its railroad network and expanding its transportation infrastructure generally, which in turn led to even greater industrial growth. Before the war, Michigan's Yankees had been instrumental in laying the foundations for the state's industrialization. After the war, with industry booming, many

Yankees gleefully took full advantage of the seemingly endless opportunities presented by Michigan's new economy.

Yankee Industry in Michigan

The industrialization of Michigan was part of the larger industrialization of the North that began in New England in the decades before the Civil War. By 1830, unlike that of the rest of the United States, the New England economy was now largely dependent on industry. There are several reasons why the Northeast industrialized in advance of the rest of the nation. One historian cites simply the Puritans, since they "created an environment in which new enterprises could flourish." The Puritans introduced the concept of stable government with a clear set of laws flexible enough to adapt to new economies as they arose. The Puritan emphasis on education, combined with the Protestant ethic, also led to the rise of a knowledgeable entrepreneurial class eager to explore new avenues of investment. The physical environment, too, played a role: New England's rocky soils were never ideal for agriculture, and many in the region had early turned instead to overseas trade, which proved to be immensely profitable and the source of capital needed for industrial investment. Moreover, with the development of agriculture in the West, New England's farmers could no longer compete, thus leaving the region with a surplus of labor looking for more profitable occupation. Finally, political events played a role. High tariffs on manufactured goods, especially on textiles and shoes, led to the local development of these industries. The Yankee mania for efficiency soon revolutionized these industries with the introduction of the "American System," a technique of mass production that centered on standardized products assembled from interchangeable parts. Subsequently applied to the manufacture of such disparate items as clocks, firearms, and steam engines, the American System led to an explosion of wildly profitable new businesses, making the per capita income in antebellum New England some 25 percent above the national average.[217] Rich New Englanders soon began to look west for new investment opportunities. Michigan, with its abundance of raw materials so necessary for the Northeast's continued industrial expansion, early became a magnet for New England capital.

The first of Michigan's natural resources to be exploited on an industrial scale was its forests. Logging had long been a mainstay of the New England

Lumbering sled in the forests of Lower Michigan. (Courtesy Archives of Michigan [neg. 01925].)

economy, and as the Yankee Diaspora moved west, so too did New England's logging industry.[218] Michigan timber, especially its great stands of white pine on the Saginaw, Muskegon, and Au Sable rivers, attracted the attention of professional logging men and their Boston and New York financiers as early as the 1830s, setting off a migration of hundreds of Maine lumberjacks to Michigan that didn't abate until after the Civil War. In Michigan, it was a Maine native, Horace Butters, who developed the timber skidding sled, and another, Winfield Gerrish, who developed the logging railroad, both of which revolutionized the logging industry and made Michigan one of the most productive logging states in the Union.[219] The logging industry catalyzed the development of towns in the hitherto sparsely populated northern counties in Lower Michigan. These were company towns, dependent on the will of a

handful of lumber barons who controlled their social and political development.[220] Reflecting typical Yankee social consciousness coupled with a desire
for a pliable workforce, many of these lumber barons took an active concern
in their towns' civic infrastructure. This included the building of schools,
churches, libraries, and hospitals, as, for example, in the lumbering towns
of Muskegon and Saginaw.

Yankee lumber barons also sought to control state politics in an effort
to protect their profits and to create smooth, if asymmetrical, relations
between labor and capital. With their immense wealth, social prestige, and
civic mindedness, the lumber interests easily dominated the legislature and
statehouse for years; beginning with the election of Massachusetts-born
Henry Crapo in 1864, five lumbermen—all of either Yankee or Yankee-Yorker
descent—would serve as Michigan's governor before 1904.[221] By this time,
Michigan lumbering was well into decline, unable to compete with the new
stands of timber now being exploited at the other end of the Yankee Diaspora
in the Pacific Northwest. Many of the lumber barons abandoned Michigan
and moved on to brighter prospects out West; a few, however, driven by a
genuine sense of social responsibility, stayed with their communities and
attempted to diversify their holdings into new and upcoming businesses.[222]

Another place Eastern Yankees looked to invest was in Michigan's Upper
Peninsula, with its abundant mineral resources. Indeed, the successful exploitation of the huge concentrations of copper and iron found there was
largely due to Yankee exploration, Yankee engineering, and, most importantly, Yankee money (an early history of the Upper Peninsula's copper
industry was entitled simply *Michigan Copper and Boston Dollars*).[223] Native
Americans had long worked the copper deposits of the Keweenaw Peninsula, but it took an 1841 report from state geologist (and Yankee-Yorker)
Douglass Houghton to set off a "copper rush." Individual prospectors soon
found that surface mining quickly played out. It was not until the 1850s that
well-financed syndicates brought intensive deep-shaft mining to the region.
Demand for copper skyrocketed with the Civil War. Nearly 70 percent of all
the copper mined in the United States during this period came from Michigan. It was during the war, too, that some of the richest copper mines were
discovered. In 1864, for example, a Connecticut Yankee, Edwin J. Hulbert,
stumbled upon what would become the fabulously productive Calumet and
Hecla mine. Developed by Quincy A. Shaw, a Harvard-educated financier

with the backing of several of Boston's richest families, the Calumet Mining Company's stock would rise 1000 percent by 1907.[224]

Iron ore was even more extensively distributed throughout the Upper Peninsula, and it too attracted Yankee money and expertise. The first great iron fields were discovered by Massachusetts-born prospector William Burt around Marquette in 1844. Again, however, it took Boston capital to mine iron on an industrial scale. The most successful of these ventures was the Cleveland-Cliffs Mining Company. In addition to making Yankees rich, industrial mining in the Upper Peninsula also brought in its wake the creation of new towns with large populations of (largely immigrant) workers and their families; this in turn led to the development of service industries, local government, schools, churches, and newspapers. William Gwinn Mather, longtime president of Cleveland-Cliffs, championed a kind of corporate paternalism toward his workers that harked back to the family-like relationships between master and employees common before the rise of the market economy. Partly this was due to his desire to forestall labor unrest, but it also evinced a genuine concern for the welfare of his workers (a concern perhaps dimly reflecting his ancestry: Mather was a lineal descendent of Massachusetts's most famous Puritan line of ministers—Richard, Increase, and Cotton Mather). William Gwinn Mather thus voluntarily instituted the eight-hour workday, worked to improve mine safety, and created a program of social benefits including pensions, accident insurance, medical care, and planned communities—all practices that other corporations would adopt in the coming years.[225] In the end, the actual number of Yankee settlers in the Upper Peninsula was quite small, but it would not be an exaggeration to say that their impact on its development—both industrial and social—was tremendous and formative.[226]

Transportation Infrastructure

All of Michigan's major industries—agriculture, mining, and lumber—depended on one thing for their success: the transportation infrastructure necessary to move raw materials to market. Here again, Boston money and Yankee know-how played a substantial part in the expansion of the state's transportation network. At its inception, the state government had attempted to fund an ambitious program of canals and railroads, but the

financial downturn of 1837 put an end to that and threatened the state with
bankruptcy; from then on, Michigan's legislators were wary of financing
such risky ventures. Ultimately, it would take private capital to complete
many of the projects the state had proposed. For example, before the Upper
Peninsula could be transformed into the great ore-producing region it would
eventually become, a convenient way around the bottleneck rapids at Sault
Ste. Marie had to be found. It was obvious that portaging huge quantities
of ore would not be feasible, but it took a Connecticut Yankee, Charles T.
Harvey, to first conceive of and then orchestrate financing for the Soo Canal
and Locks, completed in 1855.[227] The story of Michigan's railroads was also
largely a story of Yankee capital (the seminal history of this process was called
simply *Boston Capitalists and Western Railroads*).[228] In the early 1840s, two
Yankee-Yorkers, John Woods Brooks and James Frederick Joy, after much
"Yankee horsetrading," convinced the state to sell the Michigan Central
Railroad to a Boston syndicate headed by millionaire John Murray Forbes.
During the 1850s, the Michigan Central began to expand its routes and buy
up feeder lines. In time, the company became the throughway from the East
to Chicago and beyond, thus making Michigan an essential nexus on the
Midwestern railroad network.[229] The success of the Central brought in more
investors for other railroads. This, coupled with the catalyzing effect of the
Civil War, resulted in Michigan's total rail mileage rising from 779 miles in
1860 to 1,638 miles a decade later.[230]

Manufacturing: Furniture, Automobiles, and Breakfast Cereal

Given Michigan's abundance of natural materials and its growing transportation network, and given its population of skilled Yankee craftsmen and
their access to capital both from New England and from within the state, it
is not surprising that manufacturing soon joined the extractive industries
of mining and lumbering as central to the state's economy. At first, Michigan manufacturers concentrated on bulky and heavy products that were in
demand locally or regionally, but costly to import: products such as bricks,
chemicals, farm machinery, furniture, and wagons—the last two having an
especially important impact on the economic future of the state.[231] Grand
Rapids early on became a center for the furniture trade. This was due, as
one historian put it, to a confluence of "wood and waterpower" with men of

"Little Yankees" versus the Railroads

It would be a mistake to think that all of Michigan's Yankees completely embraced Michigan's new market economy or saw industrialization as an unalloyed good (Hershock 2003, x–xiii). For some, mostly small farmers and those who represented their interests, the Yankee concern for the traditional social order remained as important as the Yankee concern for profit. These "Little Yankees" saw the growth of the market and the rise of industrialization as a potential threat to their way of life. The expansion of the railroads, for example, was an especially potent symbol of the rapacity of capital: not only were the railroads chartered state monopolies with the right to set high rates and to condemn farmlands for right of ways, but the railroads also ran on the Sabbath and refused to pay full value for livestock killed on their tracks. In the summer of 1849, goaded on by anti-railroad newspaper editors such as Benjamin F. Burnett and Charles V. DeLand, Yankee farmers in Jackson County decided to take direct action, vandalizing tracks and committing sundry acts of sabotage against the hated Michigan Central. In 1850, the "Great Michigan Railroad Conspiracy" reached its climax with the derailing of an engine and the destruction by arson of the Michigan Central Depot in Detroit. Fifty men were arrested and tried for these acts, and twelve were convicted in a sensational trial that lasted four months and drew for the defense none other than William Seward, the Yankee-Yorker lawyer who would eventually become Lincoln's secretary of state. The supposed leader of the conspiracy, Yankee farmer Abel F. Fitch, died in jail awaiting trial, thus becoming for many a martyr on "the altar of freedom—a victim of injustice and oppression" of corporate greed. The spectacular nature of the attacks against the railroad and the subsequent trial undoubtedly raised the class consciousness of "Little Yankees" and solidified their resistance to the even more massive social changes they would experience due to the tremendous industrialization of the state after the Civil War (Hershock 2003, 81–92). Most "Little Yankees," however, worked within the political process to limit the power of big business in their state, both through legislation and through the revision of Michigan's constitution in 1850 and 1867. "Little Yankee" farmers also joined either the Greenback Party or the National Grange of the Patrons of Husbandry. The Grange, as it was known, was founded in 1870 by Boston-born Oliver Hudson Kelly, who, as a farmer in Minnesota, experienced some of the same frustrations as Michigan's small farmers of the era.

"entrepreneurial ambition and know-how, the latter achieved by early training, principally in New England, in the skills of joinery and cabinetmaking."[232]
Perhaps the earliest Grand Rapids furniture company to engage in mass
production and regional sales was that founded in 1847 by New Hampshire-
ites William T. Powers and E. Morris Ball in 1847. Powers and Ball pioneered
both the use of machine-made cabinetry and the then-novel sales technique
of showrooms in other cities to promote their wares. Powers and Ball were
soon joined by three other "Granite Staters," the Winchester brothers and
Charles C. Comstock, who in turn sold their businesses to the Nelson brothers of Massachusetts, thus creating the major firm of Nelson, Comstock &
Co. By 1870, eight furniture companies made Grand Rapids home and by the
turn of the century, Grand Rapids could truly claim to be "Furniture City,"
having established lucrative high-volume markets throughout the Midwest
and beyond.

Furniture manufacture would continue to be important for Michigan well
into the twentieth century, but wagon manufacture was important because it
spawned the industry that continues to dominate the state's economy to the
present day: automobiles. In the late nineteenth century, with the perfection
of steam engines and the development of gasoline engines, it was just a matter of time before they were applied to the creation of "horseless carriages."
Of course, it took considerable inventiveness to adapt these engines to create practical and affordable forms of personal transportation, but, given the
Yankee mania for productivity and efficiency, a widely recognized Yankee
trait was an inveterate inventiveness. As the Yankee Diaspora spread, so too
did the spirit of technological innovation. This is best illustrated in the life
and work of Ransom Olds.[233] Working in his father's machine shop in Lansing, Olds perfected a gasoline-fired steam engine that he then attempted to
mount in an ordinary carriage. His father was skeptical, telling one observer
that, "Ranse thinks he can put an engine in a buggy and make the contraption carry him over the roads. If he doesn't get killed at his fool undertaking,
I will be satisfied."[234] The experiment was moderately successful, but soon
Olds developed an engine that ran on gasoline alone. He patented his new
internal combustion engine in 1896 and two years later was granted the first
patent for an "automobile carriage" in the United States. The year following, the Olds Motor Vehicle Company was formed, and, at the insistence of
his investors, Olds moved his operation to Detroit, thus becoming the first

automobile firm in what would become the Motor City. It was here that Olds designed and built the immensely popular curved-dashed Oldsmobile runabout. In Detroit, too, Olds pioneered different production techniques including the use of interchangeable parts and the use of the assembly line, a technique quickly adopted and perfected by archrival, Henry Ford. The Olds Company would eventually be absorbed in 1908 by General Motors (the brainchild of Boston-born William Durant), but not before Olds had founded a new company, the REO Motor Car Company, producer of the famous REO Speedwagon, which in turn became the basis of a line of popular trucks produced until 1975. While Ransom Olds was hardly the sole inventor of the automobile, he was certainly its visionary, marrying technological innovation with new production techniques—all with a keen entrepreneurial eye to the huge industrial potential that a truly practical car represented. Others such as Henry Ford would take the industry to new heights, but it is safe to say that without Olds's example, Michigan's auto industry would have evolved very differently.

Like the automobile, ready-to-eat breakfast cereals were not invented in Michigan, but thanks to an enterprising pair of second-generation Yankee brothers—John Harvey and Will Keith Kellogg—the small Michigan town of Battle Creek would become as synonymous with the breakfast cereal industry as Detroit was with the auto industry.[235] The Kellogg brothers' story begins with the immigration of their father, John Preston Kellogg, from Hadley, Massachusetts, to Michigan Territory in 1834. Living on a farm near Battle Creek, the Kellogg family converted to Seventh-Day Adventism after the Whites relocated to Michigan in 1855. As mentioned previously, in addition to her millennial prophecies, Ellen White was beginning her emphasis on bodily purity and physical health that would soon become a hallmark of the movement. Mrs. White, always on the lookout for bright young talent to propagate her views, identified one of John Preston Kellogg's sons, John Harvey, as a likely prospect, underwriting his medical education and appointing him superintendent of the Western Health Reform Institute upon his graduation in 1876. Forceful, charismatic, and every bit as dogmatic as Mrs. White, John Harvey Kellogg gradually gained almost complete control of the institute, renaming it the Battle Creek Sanitarium and turning it into one of the premier health resorts in the world. Dr. Kellogg created a comprehensive health regimen that included vigorous exercise, the water cure, and an exclusively vegetarian diet designed according to a series of unique theories (which he communicated to the world in countless books, pamphlets, and academic papers). One of the major problems of a vegetarian diet was how to make a palatable breakfast that didn't include the American staples of fried eggs, bacon, biscuits, and gravy. To this end, Kellogg began experimenting with ready-to-eat cereal preparations, eventually developing a type of granola, wheat flakes, and corn flakes. Little did Dr. Kellogg know that his quest for vegetarianism and dietary reform would turn sleepy Battle Creek into a bustling industrial city.

As early as 1878, John Harvey Kellogg had begun retailing his breakfast foods, but his heart was never wholly into their commercialization. Dr. Kellogg, ever the purist, always considered his culinary inventions a sideline to his greater mission of health reform. Others, however, were not so chary of making money off the popularity of these new foods. One of these was an Illinois man of Yankee antecedents, C. W. Post, who came to get healthy at the "San" and stayed on in Battle Creek to make a fortune manufacturing Postum, Grape Nuts, and Post Toasties (all of which, he said, would put one "on the road to Wellville"[236]). While Post's success was somewhat irritating to John Harvey Kellogg, it was downright infuriating to his younger brother, Will Keith Kellogg. W. K. (as he was called) saw no reason to sit idly by while others got rich, for if Dr. Kellogg displayed the reform side of the Yankee personality, W. K. fully embodied the spirit of Yankee entrepreneurialism. Although he had long labored in the shadow of his famous physician brother, upon founding the Battle Creek Toasted Corn Flake Company in 1906, W. K. quickly revealed himself to be a marketing genius, not afraid to spend millions on creative advertising in order to aggressively expand his markets both at home and abroad. In addition to corn flakes, the Kellogg Company quickly began to diversify into new products and new promotions, such as premiums, prizes, and games. By 1930, W. K. had amassed so much money that he created the W. K. Kellogg Foundation to oversee the systematic disbursement of his fortune on philanthropic endeavors ranging from endowing the University of Michigan's dentistry program to building schools, hospitals, camps, and playgrounds. By the time W. K. Kellogg died at the ripe old age of ninety-one in 1951, John Harvey Kellogg and the Battle Creek Sanitarium were long just a memory; W. K.'s company, however, was now the largest manufacturer of breakfast foods in the world (with $11 billion

Dr. John Harvey Kellogg. (Courtesy of Library of Congress.)

in sales in 2006), and his foundation was surpassed in size only by the Ford and Rockefeller Foundations and the Carnegie Corporation.

Industrialization, Urbanization, and Yankee Reform

Even among those Yankees who enthusiastically celebrated Michigan's new industrial economy, many had to admit that industrialization and urbanization were changing the state's once-rural character in fundamental—and not always healthy—ways. True to Yankee form, the spirit of reform reasserted itself, although perhaps not with the white-hot intensity it had before the Civil War. If the overriding social issue confronting the country before the Civil War was slavery, the greatest social issue confronting the nation after the war was the relationship between capital and labor. Throughout the latter part of the nineteenth century—the era called the "Gilded Age"—tensions between workers and the large corporations now dominating America's economy began to rise over issues of pay, working conditions, and representation.

Eventually, such tensions produced urban unrest and, occasionally, violence. Among those working to bridge the gap between capital and labor, none worked harder or with greater moral clarity than the nation's clergy, and outstanding among this group were the Congregationalists and Unitarians who sought to adapt the old Puritan concern for the ideal social order to the present conditions of urban and industrial America.

One of the earliest of these socially concerned Congregationalists was Michigander Charles Oliver Brown, whose *Talks on the Labor Troubles* (1886) helped set the agenda for the panoply of social reforms that came to be called the Social Gospel.[237] Brown was born to immigrant New England parents in Battle Creek and was early on imbued with the spirit of reform through his father, an ardent abolitionist and temperance man. When the senior Brown marched off to the Civil War, young Charles followed, serving as valet, bugler, and eventually soldier in some of the major engagements of the conflict. During and following the war, Brown was educated at Oberlin and Olivet, where he decided to become a Congregationalist minister. Ordained in 1876, Brown served churches in Rochester, Galesburg, and Kalamazoo before following the Yankee Diaspora west to serve congregations in Dubuque, Iowa; Tacoma, Washington; and San Francisco. In Dubuque, a town undergoing rapid industrialization, Brown became increasingly concerned with growing polarization between workers and their bosses; if left unchecked, he feared, the rift would eventually destroy the fabric of America, which, he felt, would jeopardize the possibility of a just society anywhere in the world. In *Talks on the Labor Troubles,* Brown objected to the extremism of both sides: on the one hand, he rejected capitalist claims that iron economic laws made inevitable the current social situation, while on the other, he rejected the demands of socialists for the wholesale redistribution of wealth as a threat to fundamental American values. Brown's social vision, perhaps not surprisingly, harked back to New England Protestant values as embodied in the Yankee towns he knew in his youth and during his pastorate in southern Michigan. As unrealistic as this was as a solution to the labor problem, Brown's balanced diagnosis of the problem nevertheless appealed to the growing middle class within the Yankee Diaspora, making him for a time one of the foremost voices in Christian social reform in the nation.

Perhaps the most notable Yankee reformer associated with Michigan at this time—notable because she effectively combined the breadth of vision

Caroline Bartlett Crane confers with community leaders during a sanitary survey of Seattle, Washington. (Courtesy of Western Michigan University Archives and Regional History Collections.)

of Rev. Brown with a down-to-earth practicality—was Caroline Bartlett Crane.[238] Crane was born in Hudson, Wisconsin, in 1858. Thanks to her father's progressive ideas, she benefited from a thorough education, including college. Early on, Crane had become set on a career as a Unitarian minister and, after brief stints as a teacher and newspaper reporter, she was ordained and received her first pulpit, the Sioux Falls Unity Church, in 1887. Fully convinced of the importance of the Social Gospel, Crane remade the church to be more socially active and committed to social causes. Crane was next called to the Unitarian Church in Kalamazoo, which, to reflect her Social Gospel focus, she rechristened People's Church. She expanded the church to include a myriad of social programs, including a free kindergarten, home economics classes, manual arts courses, and a program for the local black community. In addition, Crane began to devote her time to other causes, such as temperance, women's suffrage, better poor relief, and a national ban on the death penalty. Crane's most innovative contribution to the Social Gospel was her application of the principles of the new science of sociology to improve the health and sanitation of local communities. Calling herself a "municipal housekeeper," Crane pioneered systematic inspection of the local food supply (especially meat and dairy), garbage collection, and water and sewer systems, and she surveyed the quality and availability of health care. National recognition soon followed, as she lobbied the state legislature and the U. S. Congress for tighter enforcement of state and federal inspection laws, and as she took inspection surveys to sixty-two cities in fourteen states. Indefatigable, Crane even tried her hand at reforming domestic architecture for the working class, creating "Everyman's House," which won first prize in the 1924 National Better Homes program. For the sheer diversity of her talents and for her ability to broaden the concerns of the Social Gospel to include nuts-and-bolts concern for some of the less glamorous aspects of urban living, Caroline Bartlett Crane was in many ways the quintessential Yankee reformer of the period.

Despite the monumental work of such Yankee reformers as Brown and Crane, it might be said that Yankee Michigan after the Civil War was increasingly torn between the "Protestant ethic" and the "spirit of capitalism," with the latter inevitably overshadowing the former. As the Puritans had always feared, money-making had become a value in and of itself, seemingly trumping all other values. Even the Yankee reforming spirit, as exemplified in Caroline Bartlett Crane, was affected by the rationalizing demands of the marketplace and the factory. From now on, most social reform would be as Crane envisioned it: professionalized and bureaucratized, the province of experts and the government, and less and less a part of any one group's cultural inheritance to be spontaneously mobilized when needed. To a great degree, Yankee identity had for nearly two centuries held in tension a set of contradictory values: the concern for individual profit and a personal concern for the social order. As the profit motive increased and social problems—especially foreign immigration—took on a perceived complexity that was beyond local solution, the strong sense of Yankee identity that had so characterized nineteenth-century Michigan began to fade. As the state prepared to enter the twentieth century, some concerned Yankees would mount concerted efforts to safeguard their cultural patrimony, but these, as we shall see, could not forestall the eclipse of Yankee identity in Michigan and the rise of a new, more useful identity, that of Midwesterner.

The Decline of Yankee Michigan

In all the states of the Middle West New England leadership . . . was marked. . . . But it must be remembered that the West itself deeply affected and even shaped these . . . forces by the influence of its own society and ideals, and that many a New England missionary of Puritan civilization became so changed by his removal as to find New England itself no longer a congenial home. There was giving as well as taking on the part of Greater New England in the West.

—Frederick Jackson Turner, "Greater New England in
the Middle of the Nineteenth Century," 1919

Despite financial success and the continuing promise of Michigan's growing economy, many of the state's Yankees began to feel a nagging sense that their social position was becoming precarious by the end of the nineteenth century. They were not alone. All of Yankeedom, it seems, was gripped by an acute anxiety that Yankees were ineluctably losing political, economic, and cultural control of their communities and regions, and thus, too, their status as a chosen people. Yankees were especially concerned by the changing nature of American society due to urbanization, industrialization, and large-scale foreign immigration. The coastal cities of New England had first experienced the brunt of these changes. Drawn by factory jobs, wave after wave of immigrants, first Irish (1840s), then French Canadians (1870s and '80s), and then southern and eastern Europeans (1890 to World War I), transformed the region in fundamental ways. In what had once been bastions of Puritanism, the largest cities on the New England seaboard, Roman Catholics were now dominant. Simultaneously, political power passed from the hands of Yankees to other ethnic groups, especially the Irish. Boston elected its first Irish mayor in 1884, and a later Irish mayor of that city claimed that, "New England is now more Irish today than any part of the world outside Ireland."[239]

In light of New England's ethnic transformation, and because of the depopulation of the New England backcountry due to migration west, some contemporary writers claimed that the Midwest was now the true seat of the old Yankee spirit. Such claims were made for Michigan specifically: W. V. Smith, for example, declared that Yankee migration had "made southern Michigan a third New England and to-day this newest New England is more exclusively of the blood of the Puritans, more representative of the ideas and ideals of the Puritans themselves than Massachusetts, than Rhode Island, than Connecticut, or any of the so called New England States of this present time."[240] Another writer said that Michigan was nothing less than "New England amended and perfected."[241] Michigan's Yankees worked hard to reinforce the historical mythology of the essential "Yankeeness" of the state, especially in the second half of the nineteenth century. Historical consciousness had always been high among Michigan's Yankees: the Historical Society of Michigan was founded by Yankees in Michigan as early as 1828, and the Detroit New England Society had been organized as early as 1844.[242] After the Civil War such historical organizations exploded, as did pioneer societies, founders' days, and founders' day picnics. Individual Yankees who could afford to began chronicling their own personal success stories in the ubiquitous county histories that began selling on a subscription basis in the 1870s.[243] Each of these brief autobiographies was a miniature sermon on the importance of Yankee discipline and grit in the settling of Michigan, and each served as a reminder of the importance of Yankee institutions for the long-term health of the state. Aimed at an even broader audience, magazine articles began appearing with titles such as "New England in Michigan" (Powell, 1896), "New England Influence in Michigan" (Williams, 1910), "The

Puritan Blood of Michigan" (Smith, 1912), "New England Men in Michigan History" (Stocking, 1921), and "The Influence of New England in Michigan" (Stevens, 1935). Much of the early *Michigan Pioneer and Historical Collections,* the premier journal of state history and forerunner to today's *Michigan History,* was devoted to documenting Yankee achievements. Articles such as "Yankee Lewis' Famous Hostelry in the Wilderness" (White, 1894) and "First 'Yankee' Family at Grand Rapids" (Baxter, 1900) were commonplace. And, in the most influential history textbook of the state, *Economic and Social Beginnings of Michigan* (1916), Professor George Fuller dogmatized that just about every good thing about Michigan was due to Yankee influence.[244]

In hindsight, it is easy to see that such Yankee boosterism was largely defensive in nature. Despite the confident claims of Yankee supremacy, it was becoming clear to many Yankees that they were no longer the sole arbiters of Michigan's future. With New England's experience in mind, Michigan's Yankees feared the erosion of their political and cultural position by the arrival of large numbers of Catholic, non-English-speaking foreigners—people, they believed, who would inevitably undermine Yankee republican and religious values.[245] With the rise of industry in Michigan, emigration from Canada and Europe accelerated tremendously, such that it accounted for about 23 percent of the state's population according to the 1880 census, and it remained this high at the 1910 census.[246] Numbers like these could not be ignored, particularly in terms of the political muscle they represented. In 1860, Yankee-dominated counties had contained 46 percent of the state's electorate, but by 1890 this had fallen to just a little less than 33 percent. Even more alarming, the Republican Party, once the staunch defender of Yankee values, was now forced to abandon some perennial Yankee issues (e.g., Sabbatarianism) and broaden its appeal to other ethnic groups in order to retain electoral majorities in the state.[247] Such demographic and political shifts, Michigan's Yankees feared, would soon be exploited by competing ethnic groups to wrest power away from them, just as had happened in the coastal cities of New England. Something, they believed, must be done.

The Revival of Yankee Nativism

Perhaps inevitably, the primary means by which Yankees throughout the Yankee Diaspora sought to retain their cultural and political hegemony was through anti-Catholic nativism. Nativism had waxed and waned throughout Yankeedom during the nineteenth century. In Michigan, it was particularly strong before the Civil War when delegates to the constitutional conventions debated limiting the franchise to American citizens, and many Yankee Michiganders had been strongly attracted to the nativist, anti-Catholic "Know Nothing" Party.[248] In the 1890s, nativism flared again in Michigan due to the perceived threat of renewed large-scale foreign immigration and fanned by an anti-Catholic crusade orchestrated by the Detroit *Patriotic American*.[249] Michigan was not alone. Anti-Catholic crusades became common in many regions of the Yankee Diaspora, and as a result two perennial nativist issues reasserted themselves: temperance and parochial schools.

Temperance, of course, had long been an issue of concern to Yankees. Yankees associated the scourge of alcoholism with the rising tide of immigration and especially with the growth of Catholic immigrants and their relaxed attitudes toward drinking on the Sabbath. As we have already seen, Michigan's Yankees made numerous attempts before the Civil War to regulate, if not stop, the liquor traffic, usually with minimal results. Late in the nineteenth century, however, beginning especially with the formation in 1896 of the Michigan branch of the Anti-Saloon League (a national organization headed by Congregationalist minister Howard Hyde Russell), Yankee sentiment for prohibition was such that, through a series of local option elections, thirty-six of Michigan's eighty-three counties became "dry" by 1910. Not surprisingly, those counties with the highest percentage of Yankee voters were the most likely to approve of prohibition.[250] In the end, so successful was this campaign for prohibition that Michigan voters approved an amendment to the state's constitution banning the manufacture and sale of liquor in 1916, a year before the Eighteenth Amendment would make prohibition the law of the land.[251]

Just as contentious, though ultimately less successful, was Michigan nativists' campaign against Catholic parochial schools. Yankees argued that public schools were necessary for the inculcation of citizenship and that parochial schools promoted social isolation and anti-democratic values. Beginning with the so-called Detroit Bible War of 1843–45 and continuing with the fight over tax support for public schools, Michigan went through cycles of conflict over public education, pitting Yankee Protestants against Catholics, usually to the detriment of the latter.[252] In the face of this, the Catholic

Church in Michigan, as it did in much of the nation, invested huge sums to create a parochial school system that would insulate Catholic children from Protestant propagandizing.[253] In response, Michigan's nativists organized the Wayne County Civic Association and launched a drive in 1916 to amend the state constitution to make public school attendance compulsory. It was not until 1920, however, that the measure finally made it to the ballot, thanks primarily to the energetic promotion of James A. Hamilton, a rising politician who wished to use the issue to win the governor's office. Campaigning for and against the amendment was bitter and occasionally violent. In the end, the Catholic Church managed to defeat the measure by effectively mobilizing its own members, as well as a coalition of Lutherans, Seventh-Day Adventists, and Christian Reformed whose own religious schools were at risk. The church nevertheless was forced to accept state oversight of its schools, and Hamilton and his allies felt there was enough support to try the amendment again. An even greater number of voters rejected the second measure, however, and in 1925 the U.S. Supreme Court ruled that a similar amendment passed in Oregon was unconstitutional, thus putting an end to further attempts by Michigan's nativists to make public school attendance compulsory.[254] Anti-Catholic nativism largely ran out of steam in Michigan at this point, so hardcore nativists began to turn their sights on a new target: the large numbers of African Americans who had joined the 1920s "Great Migration" out of the South, lured by the promise of factory jobs in places like Detroit and Dearborn.

The Fading of Yankee Ethnicity in Michigan

The importance and great irony of the revival of Yankee nativism in the 1890s and the first decades of the twentieth century is that it actually accelerated the fading of Yankee ethnicity in Michigan and throughout the Yankee Diaspora. In the fierce battles over prohibition and parochial schools, Yankee nativists found that they no longer had the numbers necessary to force the social reforms they desired. If Yankee nativists wished to win, they had to do so through alliances with like-minded English-speaking white Protestants such as transplanted Southerners, Canadian immigrants of English extraction, Scots, and, increasingly, assimilated Protestant Germans, Dutch, and Scandinavians (it should be noted that the curtailment of European immigration after World War I accelerated assimilation of these ethnic groups).[255] In the process, Yankee nativists in the Midwest helped to foster a new and more generic ethnic identity—that of the white Protestant "Midwesterner."

The general concepts of "Midwest" and "Midwesterner" were long in developing.[256] As early as the 1850s, there emerged from the states of the Old Northwest—the region that would eventually form the heart of the Midwest—a sense of regional cohesion and distinctness that some felt not only set them apart from other regions, but also allowed them to claim that they represented the future of America. Partly this was youthful hubris, but partly it was defensive, as the people of the region perceived themselves as marginalized by Eastern power brokers. In order for the region's inhabitants to exercise their rightful control over the direction of the nation (and its purse strings), regional newspaper editors and politicians sought to cultivate an autonomous "Western" identity.[257] The run up to the Civil War with its national realignment North and South interrupted this process, but once the War was won, the "Western" identity was gradually reasserted—especially as the region developed into an economic power.[258] By the turn of the century, this new regional identity—now labeled "Middle Western" or simply "Midwestern"—was firmly rooted in the minds of the region's boosters and became a byword for idealism and economic progress. Just as importantly, the label also took on powerful racial and religious connotations.[259]

The concept of "Midwest" has always been quite elastic in terms of the actual territory it covers, but the definition of a "Midwesterner" early on acquired a much more rigid and exclusivist meaning. A "Midwesterner" represented an amalgamation of the region's English-speaking white Protestants. "Midwesterner" quickly developed into a powerful regional/racial/religious identity that appealed to Yankees, since it was inclusive enough to have the political clout they craved, but still exclusive enough to rule out Indians, non-English-speaking foreigners, Catholics, Jews, and especially the region's growing population of African Americans.[260] The transition from Yankee to Midwesterner was made all the easier by the gradual loss of distinctive Yankee traits such as accent (the Yankee "twang"), the widespread adoption by non-Yankees of distinctive Yankee attitudes and practices (e.g., the Protestant ethic, the celebration of Thanksgiving, the cultivation of fruit trees, dairying, Yankee architecture, etc.), and the widespread adoption by Yankees of non-Yankee attitudes and practices (e.g., conspicuous consumption, the celebration of Christmas, etc.). Identifying with the larger white Protestant "Midwestern" majority now seemed the natural thing to do for both cultural and political reasons. Even in southern Michigan, where Yankee influence and Yankee ethnic pride had been especially strong, the Yankee ethnic label began to disappear by the first decades of the twentieth century—and this despite the best efforts of the historic preservationists mentioned previously. By mid-century, few, if any, Yankee Michiganders identified themselves as anything other than generic Midwesterners. The very idea that Yankees had once formed a distinctive and dominant ethnic culture in Michigan soon faded almost completely from popular memory.

Three Favorite Yankee Recipes

Although deserted today, Yankee Springs, halfway between Grand Rapids and Kalamazoo, was once site of the locally famous Yankee Springs Hotel. Brainchild of a genial Yankee-Yorker named William Lewis, the hotel was a magnet for travelers and settlers in the region from 1836 until Lewis's death in 1853. According to his daughter, Mary Hoyt, "it was no uncommon thing for one hundred people to tarry there for a night, while sixty teams were often stabled there between sunset and sunrise." The hotel was known especially for its extensive gardens, which spread out over four acres and produced fruit, melons, and vegetables, and for the many feasts "Yankee" Lewis organized to celebrate the holidays. Hoyt fondly remembers the first Thanksgiving there in 1838. Her "father sent out invitations to all the new settlers for miles around and later sent men and teams to gather them in." Meanwhile, her mother, Mary, roasted wild turkeys and "immense" spare ribs, which she supplemented with mince pies, pumpkin pies, and puddings. The feast was enjoyed "in a way that would astonish the dyspeptic today" (Hoyt, 1905, 292, 297).

In the spirit of "Yankee" Lewis and the hospitality of his long-vanished hotel, offered here are three favorite Yankee recipes for the desserts Mary Hoyt found on that memorable Thanksgiving table so long ago. Each of the recipes is taken (with slight modifications) from Imogene Wolcott's *The New England Yankee Cookbook* (New York: Coward-McCann, Inc., 1939).

Mincemeat Pie

3 lbs. lean beef, chopped fine

2 lbs. suet, chopped fine

3 qts. apples finely chopped

3 lbs. seeded raisins, chopped

2 lbs. currants

1 lb. citron, cut in small pieces

1 tsp. allspice

2 tsp. cinnamon

½ cup lemon juice

¼ cup orange juice

2 Tbsp. salt

4 cups sugar

1 cup coffee

2 cups cider (not too new)

1 tsp. cloves

½ cup candied orange peel, chopped

½ cup candied lemon peel, chopped

1 cup currant jelly

3 cups brandy

1 cup sherry

Mix all ingredients except brandy and sherry, and cook 2 hours; when cool, not cold, add liquor; let stand in crock for a week before using. This makes about 12 quarts and will keep indefinitely in a cool place. For pie, use 2 cups mincemeat and bake between 2 crusts.

Pumpkin Pie

1 cup steamed, strained pumpkin

⅔ cup brown sugar

½ tsp. ginger

½ tsp. salt

3 eggs, well beaten

2 cups cream (rich milk will do)

1 tsp. cinnamon

Mix all together. Pour into an unbaked pastry shell and bake in hot oven (450° F.) 10 minutes; then reduce heat to moderate (350° F.) and bake 20 to 25 minutes longer, or until knife comes out clean when inserted in custard. Makes 1 one-crust (9-inch) pie.

Baked Pudding

5 cups milk

⅔ cup dark molasses

⅓ cup granulated sugar

½ cup yellow cornmeal

1 tsp. salt

¾ cup cinnamon

⅜ cup nutmeg

4 Tbsp. butter

Heat 4 cups of the milk and add molasses, sugar, cornmeal, salt, spice, and butter to it. Cook 20 minutes or until mixture thickens. Pour into baking dish, add remaining cold milk. Do not stir. Put into slow oven (300° F.) and bake 3 hours without stirring. Serve with cream or hard sauce, or vanilla ice cream. Serves 8.

Museums, Libraries, and Archives

The following are some of the Michigan museums, libraries, and archives where further information about Yankees and their impact on the state can be found:

- **Beaver Island Historical Society,** 26275 Main St., P.O. Box 263, Beaver Island, MI 49782; (231) 448-2254
- **Burton Historical Collection,** Detroit Public Library, 5201 Woodward Ave., Detroit, MI 48202; (313) 833-1480; *www.detroitpubliclibrary.org/ burton/burton_index.htm*
- **Bentley Historical Library,** University of Michigan, 1150 Beal Ave., Ann Arbor, MI 48109-2113; (734) 764-3482; *bentley.umich.edu/*
- **Clarke Historical Library,** Central Michigan University, 250 Preston St., Central Michigan University, Mount Pleasant, MI 48859; (989) 774-3352; *clarke.cmich.edu/*
- **Detroit Historical Museum,** 5401 Woodward Avenue, Detroit, MI 48202; (313) 833-1805; *www.detroithistorical.org/*
- **Grand Army of the Republic Hall Civil War Museum,** 402 W. Michigan Ave., Marshall, MI 49069; (269) 781-8544

- **Greenfield Village,** The Henry Ford Museum, 20900 Oakwood Blvd., Dearborn, MI 48124-4088; (800) 835-5237; *www.hfmgv.org/village/default.asp*
- **Hartwick Pines Logging Museum,** Hartwick Pines State Park, 4216 Ranger Rd., Grayling, MI 49738; (989) 348-6178; *www.michigan.gov/hal /0,1607,7-160-17447_18595_18605---,00.html*
- **Historic Adventist Village,** Adventist Heritage Ministry, Historic Adventist Village Welcome Center, 411 Champion St., Battle Creek, MI 49017; (269) 965-3000; *www.adventistheritage.org/article.php?id=19*
- **Kalamazoo Valley Museum,** 230 N. Rose St., Kalamazoo, MI 49003; (800) 772-3370; *kvm.kvcc.edu/*
- **Marquette County Historical Society and Museum,** 213 N. Front St., Marquette, MI 49855; (906) 226-3571; *www.marquettecohistory.org/*
- **Marshall Historical Society and Honolulu House Museum,** 107 N. Kalamazoo Ave., Marshall, MI 49068;(269) 781-8544; *www.marshallhistoricalsociety.org/*
- **Northern Michigan University and Central Upper Peninsula Archives,** 1401 Presque Isle Ave., Marquette, MI 49855; (906) 227-1225; *www.nmu.edu/archives/*
- **Oakland County Pioneer and Historical Society,** 405 Cesar E. Chavez Ave., Pontiac, MI 48342; (248) 338-6732; *www.ocphs.org/museum.html*
- **Public Museum of Grand Rapids,** 272 Pearl St. NW, Grand Rapids, MI 49504; (616) 456-3977; *www.grmuseum.org/*
- **State Archives of Michigan, Michigan Library and Historical Center,** 702 W. Kalamazoo St., Lansing, MI 48913; (517) 373-1408; *www.michigan. gov/hal/0,1607,7-160-17445_19273_19313---,00.html*
- **Vermontville Historical Museum,** 109 N. Main St., Vermontville, MI 49096
- **Western Michigan University Archives and Regional History Collections,** Room 111, East Hall, East Campus, Western Michigan University, Kalamazoo, MI; (269) 387-8490; *www.wmich.edu/library/archives/*

Notes

1. For the most complete biography of Lyon, see Kit Lane, *Lucius Lyon: An Eminently Useful Citizen* (Douglas, Mich.: Pavilion Press, 1991).

2. Gregory S. Rose, "South Central Michigan Yankees," *Michigan History* 70, no. 2 (1986): 34; Jeremy Atack and Fred Bateman, "Yankee Farming and Settlement in the Old Northwest: A Comparative Analysis," in *Essays in the Economy of the Old Northwest,* ed. David C. Klingaman and Richard K. Vedder, 79–80 (Athens: University of Ohio Press, 1987).

3. John C. Hudson, "Yankeeland in the Middle West," *Journal of Geography* 85 (1986): 196.

4. Susan E. Gray, *The Yankee West: Community Life on the Michigan Frontier* (Chapel Hill: University of North Carolina Press, 1996); Frederick Jackson Turner, "Greater New England in the Middle of the Nineteenth Century," *American Antiquarian Society* 29 (October 15, 1919): 222–41; D. W. Meinig, *The Shaping of America: A Geographical Perspective on 500 Years of History,* vol. 2, *Continental America, 1800–1867* (New Haven, Conn.: Yale University Press, 1993), 272; Lois Kimball Mathews, *The Expansion of New England* (1909; reprin., New York: Russell and Russell, 1962); Robert Kelly, *The Cultural Pattern in American Politics* (New York: Alfred A. Knopf, 1979), 15; Hudson, "Yankeeland in the Middle West," 196.

5. Meinig, *The Shaping of America,* 272.

6. Gray, *The Yankee West,* 4–9.

7. Leonard Dinnerstein and David M. Reimers, *Ethnic Americans: A History of Immigration and Assimilation* (New York: Dodd, Mead, 1975), xiii; see also Meinig, *The Shaping of America,* 264ff.

8. Joe McCarthy, ed., *New England: Connecticut, Maine, Massachusetts, New Hampshire, Rhode Island, Vermont* (New York: Time Incorporated, 1967), 31. Another possible etymology of the word "Yankee" is that it is derived from *Jan kaas,* a Dutch epithet for New Englanders meaning "John Cheese" (Charles H. Anderson, *White Protestant Americans: From National Origins to Religious Group* [Englewood Cliffs, N.J.: Prentice-Hall, Inc., 1970], 91).

9. Quoted in Richard L. Power, *Planting Corn Belt Culture: The Impress of the Upland Southerner and Yankee in the Old Northwest* (Indianapolis: Indiana Historical Society, 1953), 19, 45–46.

10. Dixon Ryan Fox, *Yankees and Yorkers* (New York: New York University Press, 1940), 205; Van Wyck Brooks, *The World of Washington Irving* (New York: E. P. Dutton, 1944), 168n.

11. Kelly, *The Cultural Pattern in American Politics,* 15.

12. Much of the information in the following section on Puritan New England is taken from "East Anglia to Massachusetts: The Exodus of the English Puritans, 1629–41" in David Hackett Fischer, *Albion's Seed: Four British Folkways in America* (Oxford: Oxford University Press, 1989), 13–205. See also Claudia Durst Johnson, *Daily Life in Colonial New England* (Westport, Conn.: Greenwood Press, 2001).

13. Fischer, *Albion's Seed,* 13–17, 31–36.

14. Ibid., 25–31.

15. Ibid., 18–24.

16. Ibid., 112.

17. Ibid., 54, 158–59.

18. See, for example, Lewis D. Stilwell, *Migration from Vermont* (Montpelier: Vermont Historical Society, 1937), 241–42.

19. For the details of Weber's "Protestant Ethic" thesis, see Max Weber, *The Protestant Ethic and the Spirit of Capitalism* (New York: Charles Scribner's Sons, 1958).

20. Fischer, *Albion's Seed,* 132–33.

21. For an in-depth discussion of this transition, see Richard L. Bushman, *From Puritan to Yankee: Character and the Social Order in Connecticut, 1690–1765*

(Cambridge, Mass.: Harvard University Press, 1967).

22. Ibid., 288.

23. See, for example, Stilwell, *Migration from Vermont*, 242.

24. William G. McLoughlin, *Revivals, Awakenings, and Reform: An Essay on Religion and Social Change in America, 1607-1977* (Chicago: University of Chicago Press, 1978), 45-97.

25. Fox, *Yankees and Yorkers*, 3.

26. Fischer, *Albion's Seed*, 17.

27. David M. Ellis, "The Yankee Invasion of New York, 1783-1850," *New York History* 32, no. 1 (January 1951): 4-5.

28. Chard Powers Smith, *Yankees and God* (New York: Hermitage House, 1954), 300-301.

29. Fischer, *Albion's Seed*, 171-73.

30. Ellis, "The Yankee Invasion of New York," 5-9.

31. Meinig, *The Shaping of America*, 264-72.

32. Fox, *Yankees and Yorkers*, 197-98.

33. Whitney Cross, *The Burned-Over District: The Social and Intellectual History of Enthusiastic Religion in Western New York, 1800-1850* (New York: Harper Torchbooks, 1965), 3-13; McLoughlin, *Revivals, Awakenings, and Reform*, 98-131.

34. J. Harold Stevens, "The Influence of New England in Michigan," *MPHC* 19 (1935): 351.

35. George N. Fuller, "An Introduction to the Settlement of Southern Michigan from 1815 to 1835," *MPHC* 38 (1912): 543-44; Kenneth E. Lewis, *West to Far Michigan: Settling the Lower Peninsula, 1815-1860* (East Lansing: Michigan State University Press, 2002), 61; W. V. Smith, "The Puritan Blood of Michigan," *MPHC* 38 (1912): 358-59.

36. William Stocking, "New England Men in Michigan History," *Michigan History Magazine* 5, no. 1-2 (January-April 1921): 123.

37. Power, *Planting Corn Belt Culture*, 33.

38. Don Harrison Doyle, *The Social Order of a Frontier Community: Jacksonville, Illinois, 1825-70* (Urbana: University of Illinois Press, 1978), 25-28.

39. Richard L. Power, "A Crusade to Extend Yankee Culture, 1820-1865," *New England Quarterly* 12 (December 1940): 638-53.

40. Quoted in Power, *Planting Corn Belt Culture*, 8-9, 16, 19.

41. Quoted in Power, "A Crusade to Extend Yankee Culture," 647.

42. Robert W. Johnson, "Young America and the War with Mexico," in *Dueling Ea-*

gles: Reinterpreting the U.S.-Mexican War, 1846–1848, ed. Richard V. Francaviglia and Douglas W. Richmond, 164 (Fort Worth: Texas Christian University Press, 2000).

43. Nicole Etcheson, *The Emerging Midwest: Upland Southerners and the Political Culture of the Old Northwest, 1787–1861* (Bloomington: Indiana University Press, 1996), 7.

44. Doyle, *The Social Order of a Frontier Community,* 27–28.

45. Robert H. Abzug, *Cosmos Crumbling: American Reform and the Religious Imagination,* (New York: Oxford University Press, 1994), 7.

46. Stewart H. Holbrook, *The Yankee Exodus: An Account of Migration from New England* (Seattle: University of Washington Press, 1950), 81–82; J. R. Dolan, *The Yankee Peddlers of Early America* (New York: Clarkson N. Potter, Inc., 1964), 147; Willis F. Dunbar and George S. May, *Michigan: A History of the Wolverine State* (Grand Rapids, Mich.: Eerdmans, 1995), 143.

47. Dunbar and May, *Michigan,* 159–60.

48. Morris C. Taber, "New England Influence in South Central Michigan," *Michigan History* 45, no. 4 (December 1961): 306–7.

49. Holbrook, *The Yankee Exodus,* 82; Mathews, *The Expansion of New England,* 227.

50. Quoted in Pauline Joan Ullrich, "The Impact of New England Influences Upon the Formative Stages of the Non-Political Institutional Developments in Michigan During the Late Territorial Period" (Master's thesis, Wayne State University Press, 1942), 3.

51. Mathews, *The Expansion of New England,* 184; Gray, *The Yankee West,* 11.

52. Dunbar and May, *Michigan,* 157.

53. Taber, "New England Influence in South Central Michigan," 307.

54. Rose, "South Central Michigan Yankees," 32.

55. Holbrook, *The Yankee Exodus,* 87.

56. Rachel Clark, "Michigan 100 Years Ago," *Michigan History Magazine* 17 (Spring 1933): 163–74; George P. Graff, *The People of Michigan* (Lansing: Michigan Department of Education, State Library Services, 1974), 20.

57. A. B. Copley, "Early Settlement of Southwestern Michigan," *MPHC* 5 (1884): 151.

58. Dunbar and May, *Michigan,* 93.

59. Lane, *Lucius Lyon,* 128.

60. Lewis, *West to Far Michigan,* 116.

61. Malcolm J. Rohrbough, *The Trans-Appalachian Frontier: People, Societies, and*

Institutions 1775–1850 (New York: Oxford University Press, 1978), 140.

62. Stilwell, *Migration from Vermont*, 189–91.

63. George N. Fuller, *Economic and Social Beginnings of Michigan: A Study of the Settlement of the Lower Peninsula During the Territorial Period, 1805–1837* (Lansing, Mich.: Wynkoop Hallenbeck Crawford Co., 1916), 174, 315; Richard Illenden Bonner, ed., *Memoirs of Lenawee County, Michigan* (Madison, Wisc.: Western Historical Association, 1909) 61; George N. Fuller, "Settlement of Southern Michigan, 1805-1837," *MPHC* 19 (Spring-Summer 1935): 209; Stilwell, *Migration from Vermont*, 190; David Schwartz, "Duplain Township," in *History of Shiawassee and Clinton Counties, Michigan, With Illustrations and Biographical Sketches of Their Prominent Men and Pioneers*, ed. Franklin Ellis and Earl W. De La Vergne, 423-26 (Philadelphia: D. W. Ensign & Co., 1880).

64. Lewis, *West to Far Michigan*, 141–51.

65. Edward W. Barber, "The Vermontville Colony: Its Genesis and History," *MPHC* 28 (1900): 197–265; Douglas K. Meyer, "Union Colony, 1836–1870: Patterns and Process of Growth," *Vermont History* 41, no. 3 (1973); 147-57; Tabor, "New England Influence in South Central Michigan," 310.

66. Quoted in Meyer, "Union Colony," 149.

67. Ibid., 156.

68. Quoted in Justin L. Kestenbaum, ed., *The Making of Michigan 1820-1860: A Pioneer Anthology* (Detroit: Wayne State University Press, 1990), 163.

69. Gray, *The Yankee West*, 10–11.

70. Dunbar and May, *Michigan*, 165–66; Lewis, *West to Far Michigan*, 55.

71. Stilwell, *Migration from Vermont*, 135, 138, 241; Lewis, *West to Far Michigan*, 134-35; Ullrich, "The Impact of New England Influences," 4.

72. Ullrich, "The Impact of New England Influences," 3–4; Stilwell, *Migration from Vermont*, 165.

73. Rose, "South Central Michigan Yankees," 34; Atack and Bateman, "Yankee Farming and Settlement in the Old Northwest," 79-80 (cites slightly higher numbers than Rose).

74. Rose, "South Central Michigan Yankees," 34.

75. For an excellent biography of Cass, see Willard Carl Klunder, *Lewis Cass and the Politics of Moderation* (Kent, Ohio: Kent State University Press, 1996).

76. James Z. Schwartz, "Setting Boundaries and Taming Wildness: The Rise of Civic Culture on the Michigan Frontier, 1815-1840's" (Ph.D. diss., Wayne State University, 2003), 29–38.

77. Holbrook, *The Yankee Exodus,* 81.

78. Stocking, "New England Men in Michigan History," 123.

79. Taber, "New England Influence in South Central Michigan," 311; Rose, "South Central Michigan Yankees," 38–39; John W. Quist, "'The Great Majority of our Subscribers are Farmers': The Michigan Abolitionist Constituency of the 1840s," *Journal of the Early Republic* 14, no. 3 (1994): 342–44.

80. Taber, "New England Influence in South Central Michigan," 311; Mathews, *The Expansion of New England,* 223; Stevens, "The Influence of New England in Michigan," 346.

81. Thomas J. Schlereth, "The New England Presence on the Midwest Landscape," *The Old Northwest* 9, no. 2 (Summer 1983): 132; Bemis, "Local Government in Michigan and the Northwest," 14; Stevens, "The Influence of New England in Michigan," 346.

82. John G. Rice, "The Old-Stock Americans," in *They Chose Minnesota: A Survey of the State's Ethnic Groups,* ed. June Drenning Holmquist, 64 (St. Paul: Minnesota Historical Society Press, 1981).

83. Stevens, "The Influence of New England in Michigan," 346.

84. Ronald P. Formisano, *The Birth of Mass Political Parties: Michigan, 1827–1861* (Princeton, N.J.: Princeton University Press, 1971), 167.

85. For an overview of this missionary effort on Mackinac Island, see Keith R. Widder, *Battle for the Soul: Métis Children Encounter Evangelical Protestants at Mackinaw Mission, 1823–1837* (East Lansing: Michigan State University Press, 1999).

86. Ibid., 145–49.

87. John Cumming, "A Puritan Among the Chippewas," *Michigan History* 51, no. 1 (1967): 213–25; Coe Hayne, *Baptist Trail-makers in Michigan* (1936; reprin., Berrien Springs, Mich.: Hardscrabble Books, 1977).

88. Cumming, "A Puritan Among the Chippewas," 225.

89. Gray, *The Yankee West,* 73–74.

90. Ibid., 71–79.

91. Quoted in Lewis, *West to Far Michigan,* 155.

92. Quoted in Schwartz, "Setting Boundaries and Taming Wildness," 150.

93. Quoted in Klunder, *Lewis Cass and the Politics of Moderation,* 49, 51.

94. For example, see Ruth Hoppin, "Personal Recollections of Pioneer Days," *MPHC* 38 (1912): 412.

95. For a comprehensive biography of Schoolcraft, see Richard G. Bremer, *Indian*

Agent and Wilderness Scholar: The Life of Henry Rowe Schoolcraft (Mount Pleasant, Mich.: Clarke Historical Library, 1987).

96. Quoted in Lewis, *West to Far Michigan,* 82.

97. Schwartz, "Setting Boundaries and Taming Wildness," 141–42, 144.

98. Anna-Lisa Cox, *A Stronger Kinship* (New York: Little, Brown and Company, 2006), 29.

99. Lane, *Lucius Lyon,* 148–49.

100. Copley, "Early Settlement of Southwestern Michigan," 151.

101. Fuller, "Settlement of Southern Michigan," 189, 190, 194–95.

102. Formisano, *The Birth of Mass Political Parties,* 342.

103. Bruce A Rubenstein and Lawrence E. Ziewacz, *Michigan: A History of the Great Lakes State,* 3rd ed. (Wheeling, Ill.: Harlan Davidson, Inc., 2002), 74.

104. Formisano, *The Birth of Mass Political Parties,* 342.

105. Elijah Holmes Pilcher, *Protestantism in Michigan* (Detroit: R. D. S. Tyler & Co., 1878), 411; Power, *Planting Corn Belt Culture,* 140–41; Virginia E. and Robert W. McCormick, *New Englanders on the Ohio Frontier; The Migration and Settlement of Worthington, Ohio* (Kent, Ohio: Kent State University Press, 1998), 227.

106. William Nowlin, *The Bark Covered House, or Back in the Woods Again* (Detroit: Herald Publishing House, 1876), 4, 5.

107. Ibid., 11.

108. Ibid., 36; A. D. P. Van Buren, "What the Pioneers Ate and How They Fared—Michigan Food and Cookery in the Early Days," *MPHC* 5 (1884): 294.

109. A. D. P. Van Buren, "The Fever and Ague.—'Michigan Rash.'—Mosquitoes—The Old Pioneers' Foes," *MPHC* 5 (1884): 302–3.

110. Nowlin, *The Bark Covered House,* 10.

111. Melvin D. Osband, "My Recollections of Pioneers and Pioneer Life in Nankin," *MPHC* 14 (1889): 443; Van Buren, "The Fever and Ague," 302.

112. Nowlin, *The Bark Covered House,* 5, 13, 19, 38, 61.

113. Ibid., 75, 38.

114. Power, *Planting Corn Belt Culture,* 102, 104–5; Nowlin, *The Bark Covered House,* 5, 37, 74.

115. Paul E. Johnson, *The Early American Republic 1789–1829* (New York: Oxford University Press, 2007), 75; Nowlin, *The Bark Covered House,* 74.

116. Lewis, *West to Far Michigan,* 243–48.

117. Gray, *The Yankee West,* 43–65.

118. Lewis, *West to Far Michigan,* 248–49; Power, *Planting Corn Belt Culture,* 107.

119. Quoted in Johnson, *The Early American Republic*, 75.

120. Atack and Bateman, "Yankee Farming and Settlement in the Old Northwest," 92.

121. Nowlin, *The Bark Covered House*, 42.

122. Graff, *The People of Michigan*, 21.

123. Atack and Bateman, "Yankee Farming and Settlement in the Old Northwest," 94.

124. Lane, *Lucius Lyon*, 200–202.

125. Johnson, *The Early American Republic*, 73; Nowlin, *The Bark Covered House*, 43.

126. Lane, *Lucius Lyon*, 203–7.

127. Jon Gjerde, *The Minds of the West: Ethnocultural Evolution in the Rural Midwest, 1830–1917* (Chapel Hill: University of North Carolina Press, 1997), 155–56, 158, 163–64.

128. Gjerde, *The Minds of the West*, 191–94; Johnson, *The Early American Republic*, 74–75.

129. See for example Nowlin, *The Bark Covered House*, 86.

130. Gjerde, *The Minds of the West*, 168.

131. Ibid., 155–56, 198–99; Marilyn Ferris Motz, *True Sisterhood: Michigan Women and Their Kin* (Albany: State University of New York, 1983), 129.

132. Motz, *True Sisterhood*, 129.

133. Nowlin, *The Bark Covered House*, 101.

134. Gjerde, *The Minds of the West*, 197.

135. Holbrook, *The Yankee Exodus*, 85. See also Byron A. Finney, "Will Carleton, Michigan's Poet," *Michigan Historical Collections* 39 (1914): 191–203; Jerome A. Fallon, "Will Carleton: Michigan's Poet of the People," *Michigan History* 65, no. 6 (November/December 1981): 33–39.

136. W. J. Beal, "Pioneer Life in Southern Michigan in the Thirties," *MPHC* 32 (1902): 245; Ullrich, "The Impact of New England Influences," 110; A. D. P. Van Buren, "'Raisings' and 'Bees' Among the Early Settlers," *MPHC* 5 (1884): 296.

137. Johnson, *The Early American Republic*, 76.

138. Van Buren, "What the Pioneers Ate and How They Fared," 294; A. D. P. Van Buren, "The Frolics of Forty-five Years Ago," *MPHC* 5 (1884): 304*ff*; Hoppin, "Personal Recollections of Pioneer Days," 417.

139. Kestenbaum, *The Making of Michigan*, 174.

140. Fischer, *Albion's Seed*, 151.

141. Pamela Riney-Kehrberg, *Childhood on the Farm: Work, Play, and Coming of Age*

in the Midwest (Lawrence: University of Kansas Press, 2005), 38–39; Gray, *The Yankee West,* 109.

142. Van Buren, "What the Pioneers Ate and How They Fared," 294.

143. Fuller, "Settlement of Southern Michigan," 212.

144. Mary M. Hoyt, "Early Recollections of Pioneer Life in Michigan and the Founding of Yankee Springs," *MPHC* 30 (1905): 297.

145. Larry B. Massie, "When Christmas Was Just Another Day," *Michigan History* 80, no. 6 (November/December 1996): 10–15.

146. Lewis, *West to Far Michigan,* 117.

147. Fuller, "Settlement of Southern Michigan," 196.

148. Stilwell, *Migration from Vermont,* 243–44.

149. Daniel R. Campbell, "The Village and the World: The Shaping of Culture in Marshall, Michigan, 1831–1859," (Ph.D. diss., Michigan State University, 1986), 125–26; Marilyn P. Watkins, "Civilizers of the West: Clergy and Laity in Michigan Frontier Churches, 1820–1840," in *Michigan: Explorations in its Social History,* ed. Francis X. Blouin Jr. and Maris A. Vinovskis, 166–67 (Ann Arbor: Historical Society of Michigan, 1987).

150. Ullrich, "The Impact of New England Influences," 50.

151. Dunbar and May, *Michigan,* 195–96.

152. Watkins, "Civilizers of the West," 166, 167.

153. Taber, "New England Influence in South Central Michigan," 309; Stilwell, *Migration from Vermont,* 243.

154. Quoted in Ullrich, "The Impact of New England Influences," 10.

155. Meinig, *The Shaping of America,* 252–53.

156. Taber, "New England Influence in South Central Michigan," 309.

157. Beal, "Pioneer Life in Southern Michigan in the Thirties," 245.

158. Peter Temin, "The Industrialization of New England: 1830–1880," in *Engines of Enterprise: The Economic History of New England,* ed. Peter Temin, 32–33 (Cambridge, Mass.: Harvard University Press, 1999).

159. Dunbar and May, *Michigan,* 191.

160. Edward W. Bemis, "Local Government in Michigan and the Northwest," *Johns Hopkins University Studies in Historical and Political Science* 5 (March 1883): 17; Gray, *The Yankee West,* 150.

161. Dunbar and May, *Michigan,* 171; Schlereth, "The New England Presence on the Midwest Landscape," 129–30; Richard Leonard Mattson, "The Gable Front and Upright-and-Wing: An Historical Geography of Two Common American

House Types" (Ph.D. diss., University of Illinois, Urbana-Champaign, 1988),
217-21; Marshall McLennen, "Vernacular Architecture: Common House Types
in Southern Michigan," in *Michigan Folklore Reader*, ed. C. Kurt Dewhurst and
Yvonne Lockwood, 15-45 (East Lansing: Michigan State University Press, 1987).

162. For Puritan New England's ideal of the town, see Kenneth A. Lockridge, *New
England Town: The First Hundred Years, Dedham, Massachusetts, 1636-1736*
(New York: Norton, 1970).

163. Gjerde, *The Minds of the West*, 167.

164. Campbell, "The Village and the World," 30-31.

165. Ibid., 31-35, 169.

166. Ibid., 169-70.

167. Johnson, *The Early American Republic*, 115.

168. For example, see Nancy F. Cott, *The Bonds of Womanhood: "Woman's Sphere"
in New England, 1780-1835* (New Haven, Conn.: Yale University Press, 1997), 1-9,
197-200.

169. Chard Powers Smith, *Yankees and God* (New York: Hermitage House, 1954),
416.

170. Johnson, *The Early American Republic*, 114, 116-19; James D. Bratt and Christopher H. Meehan, *Gathered at the River: Grand Rapids, Michigan, and its People
of Faith* (Grand Rapids, Mich.: Eerdmans, 1993), 17-33; Martin J. Hershock, *The
Paradox of Progress: Economic Change, Individual Enterprise, and Political Culture in Michigan, 1837-1878* (Athens: Ohio University Press, 2003).

171. Riney-Kehrberg, *Childhood on the Farm*, 11-12; Campbell, "The Village and the
World," 171.

172. Willis F. Dunbar, "Early Denominational Academies and Colleges in Michigan,"
Michigan History 24 (1940): 452-53. For Sabbath schools, see Watkins, "Civiliz-
ers of the West," 165; Ullrich, "The Impact of New England Influences," 48-53;
Campbell, "The Village and the World," 82.

173. Meinig, *The Shaping of America*, 252.

174. Taber, "New England Influence in South Central Michigan," 309-10.

175. Ullrich, "The Impact of New England Influences," 36-38, 46.

176. Campbell, "The Village and the World," 69-84.

177. Ullrich, "The Impact of New England Influences," 65-71, 72-87; Campbell, "The
Village and the World," 85, 112-15; Roger L. Rosentreter, "Eaton County," *Michigan History* 66, no. 1 (January/February 1982): 11.

178. Daniel F. Ring, "Outpost of New England Culture: The Ladies' Library Associa-

tion of Kalamazoo, Michigan," *Libraries and Culture* 32, no. 1 (1997): 38–39, 42.

179. Formisano, *The Birth of Mass Political Parties*, 83.

180. Bratt and Meehan, *Gathered at the River*, 17–33.

181. Curtis B. Johnson, *Islands of Holiness: Rural Religion in Upstate New York, 1790–1860* (Ithaca, N.Y.: Cornell University Press, 1989), 67–68; Johnson, *The Early American Republic*, 119.

182. George N. Fuller, *Michigan: A Centennial History of the State and Its People*, vol. 2 (Chicago, Ill.: Lewis Publishing Co., 1939), 514; Margaret B. Macmillan, *The Methodist Church in Michigan*, vol. 1 (Grand Rapids, Mich.: Eerdmans, 1967), 307–11.

183. Dunbar, "Early Denominational Academies," 451–66.

184. For a good introduction to Mormonism, see Jan Shipps, *Mormonism: The Story of a New Religious Tradition* (Urbana: University of Illinois Press, 1987).

185. John Cumming and Audrey Cumming, "The Saints Come to Michigan," *Michigan History* 49 (March 1965): 13–15.

186. For book-length studies of Strang and the Mormons of Beaver Island, see Roger Van Nord, *King of Beaver Island: The Life and Assassination of James Jesse Strang* (Champaign: University of Illinois Press, 1988) and Vickie Cleverley Speek, *"God Has Made Us a Kingdom": James Strang and the Midwest Mormons* (Salt Lake City: Signature Books, 2006).

187. For a good introduction to the history of Seventh-Day Adventism, see Gary Land, ed., *Adventism in America: A History* (Berrien Springs, Mich.: Andrews University Press, 1998).

188. Quoted in Le Roy Barrett, "Never on Sunday," *Michigan History Magazine* 90, no. 4 (July/August, 2006): 18.

189. Formisano, *The Birth of Mass Political Parties*, 123–24.

190. Barrett, "Never on Sunday," 19.

191. Hershock, *The Paradox of Progress*, 106.

192. Kestenbaum, *The Making of Michigan*, 325.

193. Hershock, *The Paradox of Progress*, 105, 106.

194. Formisano, *The Birth of Mass Political Parties*, 233.

195. Kestenbaum, *The Making of Michigan*, 73.

196. Rubenstein and Ziewacz, *Michigan*, 91.

197. Quoted in Floyd Benjamin Streeter, *Political Parties in Michigan 1837–1860* (Lansing: Michigan Historical Commission, 1918), 48, 49.

198. Ibid., 50–53.

199. Ball, *Born to Wander*, 26.

200. Ronald P. Formisano, "The Edge of Caste: Colored Suffrage in Michigan, 1827–1861," *Michigan History* 56, no. 1 (1972): 24–25, 29.

201. Hershock, *The Paradox of Progress*, 207.

202. Quoted in Formisano, *The Birth of Mass Political Parties*, 153; Formisano, "The Edge of Caste," 25–26, 33.

203. Laura S. Haviland, *Woman's Life-Work: Including Thirty Years' Service on the Underground Railroad and in the War* (Grand Rapids, Mich.: S. B. Shaw, 1881).

204. Hershock, *The Paradox of Progress*, xii.

205. Formisano, *The Birth of Mass Political Parties*, 61–62, 128–36.

206. Rubenstein and Ziewacz, *Michigan*, 100–103.

207. Formisano, *The Birth of Mass Political Parties*, 295; Robert Kelly, *The Cultural Pattern in American Politics* (New York: Alfred A. Knopf, 1979), 200.

208. Harriette M. Dilla, *The Politics of Michigan, 1865-1878* (1912; reprin., New York: AMS Press, 1970), 71.

209. Frank B. Woodford, *Father Abraham's Children: Michigan Episodes in Civil War* (Detroit: Wayne State University Press, 1999), 167–76; Paul D. Mehney, "Capturing a Confederate," *Michigan History Magazine* 84, no. 3 (May/June 2000): 42–49.

210. Quoted in Dunbar and May, *Michigan*, 319. For a narrative of Blair's career, see Jean Joy L. Fennimore, "Austin Blair: Pioneer Lawyer, 1818-1844," *Michigan History* 48, no. 1 (1964a): 1–17 and "Austin Blair: Political Idealist, 1845-1860" *Michigan History* 48, no. 2 (1964b): 130–166.

211. Quoted in Roger L. Rosentreter, "We Are Coming Father Ab'ram: Michigan in the Civil War," *Michigan History* 67, no. 3 (May/June 1983): 35.

212. Rubenstein and Ziewacz, *Michigan*, 108.

213. For a biography of Chandler, see Wilmer C. Harris, *Public Life of Zachariah Chandler, 1851-1875* (Lansing: Michigan Historical Commission, 1917).

214. Quoted in Hershock, *The Paradox of Progress*, 163.

215. Kelly, *The Cultural Pattern in American Politics*, 248.

216. Albert A. Blum, "Guns, Grain and Iron Ore: Michigan's Economy during the Civil War," *Michigan History* 69, no. 3 (May/June 1985): 13–20.

217. Temin, "The Industrialization of New England," 3, 37.

218. Jeremy W. Kilar, *Michigan's Lumbertowns: Lumbermen and Laborers in Saginaw, Bay City, and Muskegon, 1870-1905* (Detroit: Wayne State University Press, 1990), 138.

219. Holbrook, *The Yankee Exodus,* 85–86; Dunbar and May, *Michigan,* 342; Russell M. Magnaghi, "Yankee Influence in Michigan's Upper Peninsula" (unpublished paper, Central Upper Peninsula and Northern Michigan University Archives, 1999), 23. It should be noted that Michigan's logging boom also stimulated much foreign immigration, including large numbers of Canadians.

220. Kilar, *Michigan's Lumbertowns,* 135–63.

221. Dunbar and May, *Michigan,* 332, 348; Kilar, *Michigan's Lumbertowns,* 158, 237.

222. Kilar, *Michigan's Lumbertowns,* 260–96.

223. William B. Gates, *Michigan Copper and Boston Dollars: An Economic History of the Michigan Copper Mining Industry* (Cambridge, Mass.: Harvard University Press, 1951).

224. Rubenstein and Ziewacz, *Michigan,* 80, 116.

225. Burton H. Boyum, "William Gwinn Mather," *Michigan History* 78, no. 6 (1994): 77–79.

226. For a comprehensive overview of the Yankee impact on the development of the Upper Peninsula, see Magnaghi, "Yankee Influence in Michigan's Upper Peninsula," 1–34.

227. Dunbar and May, *Michigan,* 259–62; Holbrook, *The Yankee Exodus,* 90.

228. Arthur M. Johnson and Barry E. Supple, *Boston Capitalists and Western Railroads: A Study in the Nineteenth-Century Railroad Investment Process* (Cambridge, Mass.: Harvard University Press, 1967).

229. Graydon M. Meints, "Michigan's Main Line," *Michigan History* 77 no. 6 (1993): 12, 13–14.

230. Hershock, *The Paradox of Progress,* 197.

231. David Meyer, "The Roots of American Industrialization, 1790–1860," EH.Net Encyclopedia, ed. Robert Whaples (May 13, 2004). URL: eh.net/encyclopedia/article/meyer.industrialization (accessed March 3, 2006), 9.

232. James Stanford Bradshaw, "Grand Rapids Furniture Beginnings," *Michigan History* 52, no. 4 (1968): 279–98.

233. For an excellent biography of Ransom Olds, see George S. May, *R. E. Olds: Auto Industry Pioneer* (Grand Rapids, Mich.: Eerdmans, 1977).

234. Ibid., 47.

235. Gerald Carson, *Cornflake Crusade: From the Pulpit to the Breakfast Table* (New York: Rinehart and Co., 1957), 71–256.

236. Ibid., 162.

237. Dewey D. Wallace, Jr., "Charles Oliver Brown at Dubuque: A Study in the Ideals

of Midwestern Congregationalist in the Late Nineteenth Century," *Church History* 53, no. 1 (March 1984): 46–60.

238. O'Ryan Rickard, *A Just Verdict: The Life of Caroline Bartlett Crane* (Kalamazoo, Mich.: New Issues Press, 1994).

239. Quoted in Joseph A. Conforti, *Imagining New England: Explorations of Regional Identity from the Pilgrims to the Mid-Twentieth Century* (Chapel Hill: University of North Carolina Press, 2001), 209; Turner, "Greater New England in the Middle of the Nineteenth Century," 226–27.

240. Smith, "The Puritan Blood of Michigan," 360.

241. E. P. Powell, "New England in Michigan," *New England Magazine* 13 (September 1895–February 1896): 427.

242. Ullrich, "The Impact of New England Influences," 83; Stevens, "The Influence of New England in Michigan," 341; Stocking, "New England Men in Michigan History," 136.

243. Anna-Lisa Cox, "A Covert from Storm: Race, Rights and Community in Nineteenth-Century Rural Michigan" (Ph.D. diss., University of Illinois, Urbana-Champaign, 2002), 197.

244. See, for example, Fuller, *Economic and Social Beginnings of Michigan,* 213–14.

245. Schwartz, "Setting Boundaries and Taming Wildness," 59.

246. Andrew D. Perejda, "Sources and Dispersal of Michigan's Population," *Michigan History* 32 (1948): 356, 358.

247. Paul Kleppner, *The Cross of Culture: A Social Analysis of Midwestern Politics, 1850–1900* (New York: Free Press, 1970), 16, 110*ff.*

248. Formisano, *The Birth of Mass Political Parties,* 91–95, 247–65.

249. Donald L. Kinser, "The Political Uses of Anti-Catholicism: Michigan and Wisconsin, 1890–1894," *Michigan History* 39, no. 3 (September 1955): 313–15.

250. Larry Engelmann, "Dry Renaissance: The Local Option Years, 1889–1917," *Michigan History* 59 (1975): 73–74, 76; Dunbar and May, *Michigan,* 469–70.

251. Rubenstein and Ziewacz, *Michigan,* 219–20.

252. David L. Angus, "Detroit's Great School Wars: Religion and Politics in a Frontier City, 1842–1853," *Michigan Academician* 12, no. 3 (1980): 261–80; Formisano, *The Birth of Mass Political Parties,* 220–27.

253. For the development of the Catholic parochial school system in Detroit, see JoEllen McNergney Vinyard, *For Faith and Fortune: The Education of Catholic Immigrants in Detroit, 1805–1925* (Urbana: University of Illinois Press, 1998).

254. Thomas Elton Brown, "Patriotism or Religion: Compulsory Public Education

and Michigan's Roman Catholic Church, 1920-1924," *Michigan History* 64, no. 4 (July/August 1980): 36–42.

255. Anderson, *White Protestant Americans,* 112; Andrew R. L. Cayton and Susan E. Gray, ed., *The American Midwest: Essays on Regional History* (Bloomington: Indiana University Press, 2001), 23.

256. James R. Shortridge, *The Middle West: Its Meaning in American Culture* (Lawrence: University of Kansas Press, 1989).

257. Cayton and Gray, *The American Midwest,* 9–10; Power, *Planting Corn Belt Culture,* 162–68.

258. Etcheson, *The Emerging Midwest,* 1–2; Cayton and Gray, *The American Midwest,* 17–22.

259. Cayton and Gray, *The American Midwest,* 23–26; Power, *Planting Corn Belt Culture,* 136–41, 174.

260. Cayton and Gray, *The American Midwest,* 24–25.

For Further Reference

MPHC = Michigan Pioneer and Historical Collections

Abzug, Robert H. *Cosmos Crumbling: American Reform and the Religious Imagination.* New York: Oxford University Press, 1994.

Anderson, Charles H. *White Protestant Americans: From National Origins to Religious Group.* Englewood Cliffs, N.J.: Prentice-Hall, Inc., 1970.

Angus, David L. "Detroit's Great School Wars: Religion and Politics in a Frontier City, 1842–1853," *Michigan Academician* 12, no. 3 (1980): 261–80.

Asher, Robert. "Connecticut Inventors," www.ctheritage.org/encyclopedia/topical-surveys/inventors.htm (accessed June 8, 2007).

Atack, Jeremy, and Fred Bateman. "Yankee Farming and Settlement in the Old Northwest: A Comparative Analysis." In *Essays in the Economy of the Old Northwest,* edited by David. C. Klingman and Richard K. Vedder, 77–102. Athens, Ohio: University of Ohio Press, 1987.

Ball, John. *Born to Wander: The Autobiography of John Ball.* Grand Rapids, Mich.: Grand Rapids Historical Commission, 1994.

Barber, Edward W. "The Vermontville Colony: Its Genesis and History." *MPHC* 28 (1900): 197–265.

Barrett, Le Roy. "Never on Sunday." *Michigan History Magazine* 90, no. 4 (July/August 2006): 16–23.

Baxter, Albert. "First 'Yankee' Family at Grand Rapids." *MPHC* 29 (1899–1900): 503–5.

Beal, W. J. "Pioneer Life in Southern Michigan in the Thirties." *MPHC* 32 (1902): 236–46.

Bemis, Edward W. "Local Government in Michigan and the Northwest." *Johns Hopkins University Studies in Historical and Political Science* 5 (March 1883): 5–25.

Berry, Chad Thomas. "Social Highways: Southern White Migration to the Midwest, 1910–1990." Ph.D. diss., Indiana University, 2005.

Blum, Albert A. "Guns, Grain and Iron Ore: Michigan's Economy during the Civil War." *Michigan History* 69, no. 3 (May/June 1985): 13–20.

Bonner, Richard Illenden, ed. *Memoirs of Lenawee County, Michigan.* Madison, Wisc.: Western Historical Association, 1909.

Boyum, Burton H. "William Gwinn Mather." *Michigan History* 78, no. 6 (1994): 77–79.

Bradshaw, James Stanford. "Grand Rapids Furniture Beginnings." *Michigan History* 52, no. 4 (1968): 279–98.

Bratt, James D., and Christopher H. Meehan. *Gathered at the River: Grand Rapids, Michigan, and its People of Faith.* Grand Rapids, Mich.: Eerdmans, 1993.

Bremer, Richard G. *Indian Agent and Wilderness Scholar: The Life of Henry Rowe Schoolcraft.* Mount Pleasant, Mich.: Clarke Historical Library, 1987.

Brooks, Van Wyck. *The World of Washington Irving.* New York: E. P. Dutton, 1944.

Brown, Thomas Elton. "Patriotism or Religion: Compulsory Public Education and Michigan's Roman Catholic Church, 1920–1924." *Michigan History* 64, no. 4 (July/August 1980): 36–42.

Bushman, Richard L. *From Puritan to Yankee: Character and the Social Order in Connecticut, 1690–1765.* Cambridge, Mass.: Harvard University Press, 1967.

Campbell, Daniel R. "The Village and the World: The Shaping of Culture in Marshall, Michigan, 1831–1859." Ph.D. diss., Michigan State University, 1986.

Carleton, Will. *Farm Ballads.* New York: Harper and Brothers, 1873.

Carson, Gerald. *Cornflake Crusade: From the Pulpit to the Breakfast Table.* New York: Rinehart and Co., 1957.

Cayton, Andrew R. L., and Susan E. Gray, eds. *The American Midwest: Essays on Regional History.* Bloomington: Indiana University Press, 2001.

Clark, Rachel. "Michigan 100 Years Ago," *Michigan History Magazine* 17 (Spring 1933): 163–74.

Conforti, Joseph A. *Imagining New England: Explorations of Regional Identity from the Pilgrims to the Mid-Twentieth Century.* Chapel Hill: University of North Carolina Press, 2001.

Copley, A. B. "Early Settlement of Southwestern Michigan." *MPHC* 5 (1884): 144–51.

Cott, Nancy F. *The Bonds of Womanhood: "Woman's Sphere" in New England, 1780–1835.* New Haven, Conn.: Yale University Press, 1997.

Cox, Anna-Lisa. "A Covert from Storm: Race, Rights and Community in Nineteenth-Century Rural Michigan." Ph.D. diss., University of Illinois, Urbana-Champaign, 2002.

———. *A Stronger Kinship.* New York: Little, Brown and Company, 2006.

Cross, Whitney. *The Burned-Over District: The Social and Intellectual History of Enthusiastic Religion in Western New York, 1800–1850.* New York: Harper Torchbooks, 1965.

Cumming, John. "A Puritan Among the Chippewas." *Michigan History* 51, no. 1 (1967): 213–25.

Cumming, John, and Audrey Cumming. "The Saints Come to Michigan." *Michigan History* 49 (March 1965): 12–27.

Dilla, Harriette M. *The Politics of Michigan, 1865–1878.* 1912; reprin., New York: AMS Press, 1970.

Dinnerstein, Leonard, and David M. Reimers. *Ethnic Americans: A History of Immigration and Assimilation.* New York: Dodd, Mead, 1975.

Dolan, J. R. *The Yankee Peddlers of Early America.* New York: Clarkson N. Potter, Inc., 1964.

Doyle, Don Harrison. *The Social Order of a Frontier Community: Jacksonville, Illinois, 1825–70.* Urbana, Ill.: University of Illinois Press, 1978.

Dunbar, Willis F. "Early Denominational Academies and Colleges in Michigan," *Michigan History* 24 (1940): 451–66.

Dunbar, Willis F., and George S. May. *Michigan: A History of the Wolverine State.* Grand Rapids, Mich.: Eerdmans, 1995.

Ellis, David M. "The Yankee Invasion of New York, 1783–1850." *New York History* 32, no. 1 (January 1951): 3–18.

Engelmann, Larry. "Dry Renaissance: The Local Option Years, 1889–1917." *Michigan History* 59 (1975): 69–90.

Etcheson, Nicole. *The Emerging Midwest: Upland Southerners and the Political Culture of the Old Northwest, 1787–1861.* Bloomington: Indiana University Press, 1996.

Fallon, Jerome A. "Will Carleton: Michigan's Poet of the People." *Michigan History* 65, no. 6 (November/December 1981): 33–39.

Farmer, Silas. *History of Detroit and Wayne County and Early Michigan.* Detroit, Mich.: Silas Farmer and Co., 1890.

Fennimore, Jean Joy L. "Austin Blair: Pioneer Lawyer, 1818–1844." *Michigan History*

48, no. 1 (1964a): 1–17.

———. "Austin Blair: Political Idealist, 1845–1860." *Michigan History* 48, no. 2 (1964b): 130–166.

Finney, Byron A. "Will Carleton, Michigan's Poet." *Michigan Historical Collections* 39 (1914): 191–203.

Fischer, David Hackett. *Albion's Seed: Four British Folkways in America.* Oxford: Oxford University Press, 1989.

Formisano, Ronald P. *The Birth of Mass Political Parties: Michigan, 1827–1861.* Princeton, N.J.: Princeton University Press, 1971.

———. "The Edge of Caste: Colored Suffrage in Michigan, 1827-1861." *Michigan History* 56, no. 1 (1972): 19-41.

Fox, Dixon Ryan. *Yankees and Yorkers.* New York: New York University Press, 1940.

Fuller, George N. "An Introduction to the Settlement of Southern Michigan from 1815 to 1835." *MPHC* 38 (1912): 538–79.

———. *Economic and Social Beginnings of Michigan: A Study of the Settlement of the Lower Peninsula During the Territorial Period, 1805–1837.* Lansing, Mich.: Wynkoop Hallenbeck Crawford Co., 1916.

———. "Settlement of Southern Michigan, 1805–1837," *MPHC* 19 (Spring–Summer 1935): 179–214.

———. *Michigan: A Centennial History of the State and Its People.* Vol. 2. Chicago, Ill.: Lewis Publishing Co., 1939.

Gates, William B. *Michigan Copper and Boston Dollars: An Economic History of the Michigan Copper Mining Industry.* Cambridge, Mass.: Harvard University Press, 1951.

Genser, Wallace. "'A Rigid Government Over Ourselves': Transformations in Ethnic, Gender, and Race Consciousness on the Northern Borderlands—Michigan, 1805–1865." Ph.D. diss., University of Michigan, 1998.

Gjerde, Jon. *The Minds of the West: Ethnocultural Evolution in the Rural Midwest, 1830–1917.* Chapel Hill: University of North Carolina Press, 1997.

Graff, George P. *The People of Michigan.* Lansing: Michigan Department of Education, State Library Services, 1974.

Gray, Susan E. *The Yankee West: Community Life on the Michigan Frontier.* Chapel Hill: University of North Carolina Press, 1996.

Harris, Wilmer C. *Public Life of Zachariah Chandler, 1851–1875.* Lansing: Michigan Historical Commission, 1917.

Haviland, Laura S. *A Woman's Life-Work: Including Thirty Years' Service on the Un-*

derground Railroad and in the War. Grand Rapids, Mich.: S. B. Shaw, 1881.

Hayne, Coe. *Baptist Trail-makers in Michigan.* 1936; reprin., Berrien Springs, Mich.: Hardscrabble Books, 1977.

Hershock, Martin J. *The Paradox of Progress: Economic Change, Individual Enterprise, and Political Culture in Michigan, 1837–1878.* Athens: Ohio University Press, 2003.

Holbrook, Stewart H. *The Yankee Exodus: An Account of Migration from New England.* Seattle: University of Washington Press, 1950.

Hoppin, Ruth. "Personal Recollections of Pioneer Days." *MPHC* 38 (1912): 410–16.

Hoyt, Mary M. "Early Recollections of Pioneer Life in Michigan and the Founding of Yankee Springs." *MPHC* 30 (1905): 289–302.

Hudson, John C. "Yankeeland in the Middle West." *Journal of Geography* 85 (1986): 195–200.

Hurd, Philo R. "An Historical Sketch of Congregationalism in Michigan, Brought Down to the Year 1884," *MPHC* 7 (1886): 103–11.

Johnson, Arthur M., and Barry E. Supple. *Boston Capitalists and Western Railroads. A Study in the Nineteenth-Century Railroad Investment Process.* Cambridge, Mass.: Harvard University Press, 1967.

Johnson, Claudia Durst. *Daily Life in Colonial New England.* Westport, Conn.: Greenwood Press, 2001.

Johnson, Curtis D. *Islands of Holiness: Rural Religion in Upstate New York, 1790–1860.* Ithaca, N.Y.: Cornell University Press, 1989.

Johnson, Paul E. *The Early American Republic 1789–1829.* New York: Oxford University Press, 2007.

Johnson, Robert W. "Young America and the War with Mexico." In *Dueling Eagles: Reinterpreting the U.S.-Mexican War, 1846–1848,* edited by Richard V. Francaviglia and Douglas W. Richmond, 155–76. Fort Worth: Texas Christian University Press, 2000.

Kelly, Robert. *The Cultural Pattern in American Politics.* New York: Alfred A. Knopf, 1979.

Kestenbaum, Justin L., ed. *The Making of Michigan 1820–1860: A Pioneer Anthology.* Detroit, Mich.: Wayne State University Press, 1990.

Kilar, Jeremy W. *Michigan's Lumbertowns: Lumbermen and Laborers in Saginaw, Bay City, and Muskegon, 1870–1905.* Detroit, Mich.: Wayne State University Press, 1990.

Kinser, Donald L. "The Political Uses of Anti-Catholicism: Michigan and Wisconsin,

1890–1894." *Michigan History* 39, no. 3 (September 1955): 312–26.

Kleppner, Paul. *The Cross of Culture: A Social Analysis of Midwestern Politics, 1850–1900*. New York: Free Press, 1970.

Klunder, Willard Carl. *Lewis Cass and the Politics of Moderation*. Kent, Ohio: Kent State University Press, 1996.

Kuhns, Frederick Irving. "The Breakup of the Plan of Union in Michigan." *Michigan History* 32 (June 1948): 157–80.

Land, Gary, ed. *Adventism in America: A History*. Berrien Springs, Mich.: Andrews University Press, 1998.

Lane, Kit. *Lucius Lyon: An Eminently Useful Citizen*. Douglas, Mich.: Pavilion Press, 1991.

Lewis, Kenneth E. *West to Far Michigan: Settling the Lower Peninsula, 1815–1860*. East Lansing: Michigan State University Press, 2002.

Lockridge, Kenneth A. *New England Town: The First Hundred Years, Dedham, Massachusetts, 1636–1736*. New York: Norton, 1970.

Ludlum, David M. *Social Ferment in Vermont 1791–1850*. New York: AMS Press, Inc., 1966.

Macmillan, Margaret B. *The Methodist Church in Michigan*. Vol. 1 and 2. Grand Rapids, Mich.: Eerdmans, 1967.

Magnaghi, Russell M. "Yankee Influence in Michigan's Upper Peninsula." Unpublished paper, Central Upper Peninsula and Northern Michigan University Archives, 1999, 1–34.

March, Walter. *Shoepac Recollections: A Wayside Glimpse of American Life*. New York: Bunce and Brother, Publishers, 1856.

Massie, Larry B. "When Christmas Was Just Another Day." *Michigan History* 80, no. 6 (November/December 1996): 10–15.

Mathews, Lois Kimball. *The Expansion of New England*. 1909; New York: Russell and Russell, 1962.

Mattson, Richard Leonard. "The Gable Front and Upright-and-Wing: An Historical Geography of Two Common American House Types." Ph.D. diss., University of Illinois, Urbana-Champaign, 1988.

May, George S. *R. E. Olds: Auto Industry Pioneer*. Grand Rapids, Mich.: Eerdmans, 1977.

McCarthy, Joe, ed. *New England: Connecticut, Maine, Massachusetts, New Hampshire, Rhode Island, Vermont*. New York: Time Incorporated, 1967.

McCormick, Virginia E., and Robert W. McCormick. *New Englanders on the Ohio*

Frontier: The Migration and Settlement of Worthington, Ohio. Kent, Ohio: Kent State University Press, 1998.

McLennen, Marshall. "Vernacular Architecture: Common House Types in Southern Michigan." In *Michigan Folklore Reader,* edited by C. Kurt Dewhurst and Yvonne Lockwood, 15–45. East Lansing: Michigan State University Press, 1987.

McLoughlin, William G. *Revivals, Awakenings, and Reform: An Essay on Religion and Social Change in America, 1607–1977.* Chicago, Ill.: University of Chicago Press, 1978.

Mehney, Paul D. "Capturing a Confederate." *Michigan History Magazine* 84, no. 3 (May/ June 2000): 42–49.

Meinig, D. W. *The Shaping of America: A Geographical Perspective on 500 Years of History.* Vol. 2, *Continental America, 1800–1867.* New Haven, Conn.: Yale University Press, 1993.

Meints, Graydon M. "Michigan's Main Line." *Michigan History* 77, no. 6 (1993): 12–28.

Meyer, David. "The Roots of American Industrialization, 1790–1860." EH.Net Encyclopedia, edited by Robert Whaples (May 13, 2004), pp. 1–12. URL: eh.net/encyclopedia/article/meyer.industrialization (accessed March 3, 2006).

Meyer, Douglas K. "Union Colony, 1836–1870: Patterns and Process of Growth." *Vermont History* 41, no. 3 (1973): 147–57.

Motz, Marilyn Ferris. *True Sisterhood: Michigan Women and Their Kin.* Albany: State University of New York, 1983.

Nowlin, William. *The Bark Covered House, or Back in the Woods Again.* Detroit, Mich: Herald Publishing House, 1876.

Osband, Melvin D. "My Recollections of Pioneers and Pioneer Life in Nankin." *MPHC* 14 (1889): 431–83.

Perejda, Andrew D. "Sources and Dispersal of Michigan's Population." *Michigan History* 32 (1948): 355–66.

Pierce, John D. "Congregationalism in Michigan." *MPHC* 12 (1888): 351–61.

Pilcher, Elijah Holmes. *Protestantism in Michigan.* Detroit, Mich.: R. D. S. Tyler & Co., 1878.

Powell, E. P. "New England in Michigan." *New England Magazine* 13 (September 1895–February 1896): 419–28.

Power, Richard L. "A Crusade to Extend Yankee Culture, 1820–1865." *New England Quarterly* 12 (December 1940): 638–53.

———. *Planting Corn Belt Culture: The Impress of the Upland Southerner and Yankee in the Old Northwest.* Indianapolis: Indiana Historical Society, 1953.

Quist, John W. "'The Great Majority of our Subscribers are Farmers': The Michigan Abolitionist Constituency of the 1840s." *Journal of the Early Republic* 14, no. 3 (1994): 324–58.

Rice, John G. "The Old-Stock Americans." In *They Chose Minnesota: A Survey of the State's Ethnic Groups*, edited by June Drenning Holmquist, 55–72. St. Paul: Minnesota Historical Society Press, 1981.

Rickard, O'Ryan. *A Just Verdict: The Life of Caroline Bartlett Crane*. Kalamazoo, Mich.: New Issues Press, 1994.

Riney-Kehrberg, Pamela. *Childhood on the Farm: Work, Play, and Coming of Age in the Midwest*. Lawrence: University of Kansas Press, 2005.

Ring, Daniel F. "Outpost of New England Culture: The Ladies' Library Association of Kalamazoo, Michigan." *Libraries and Culture* 32, no. 1 (1997): 38–56.

Rohrbough, Malcolm J. *The Trans-Appalachian Frontier: People, Societies, and Institutions 1775–1850*. New York: Oxford University Press, 1978.

Rose, Gregory S. "South Central Michigan Yankees." *Michigan History* 70, no. 2 (1986): 32–39.

Rosentreter, Roger L. "Eaton County." *Michigan History* 66, no. 1 (January/February 1982): 8–11.

———. "We Are Coming Father Ab'ram: Michigan in the Civil War." *Michigan History* 67, no. 3 (May/June 1983): 34–42.

Rubenstein, Bruce A., and Lawrence E. Ziewacz. *Michigan: A History of the Great Lakes State*. 3rd ed. Wheeling, Ill.: Harlan Davidson, Inc., 2002.

Sanderson, J. P. "Congregationalism as a Factor in the Making of Michigan." *Michigan History* 2 (January 1918): 143–53.

Schlereth, Thomas J. "The New England Presence on the Midwest Landscape." *The Old Northwest* 9, no. 2 (Summer 1983): 125–42.

Schwartz, David. "Duplain Township." In *History of Shiawassee and Clinton Counties, Michigan, With Illustrations and Biographical Sketches of Their Prominent Men and Pioneers*, edited by Franklin Ellis and Earl W. De La Vergne, 421–33. Philadelphia: D. W. Ensign & Co., 1880.

Schwartz, James Z. "Setting Boundaries and Taming Wildness: The Rise of Civic Culture on the Michigan Frontier, 1815–1840's." Ph.D. diss., Wayne State University, 2003.

Shipps, Jan. *Mormonism: The Story of a New Religious Tradition*. Urbana: University of Illinois Press, 1987.

Shortridge, James R. *The Middle West: Its Meaning in American Culture*. Lawrence:

University of Kansas Press, 1989.

Smith, Chard Powers. *Yankees and God.* New York: Hermitage House, 1954.

Smith, W. V. "The Puritan Blood of Michigan." *MPHC* 38 (1912): 355–61.

Speek, Vickie Cleverley. *"God Has Made Us a Kingdom": James Strang and the Midwest Mormons.* Salt Lake City, Utah: Signature Books, 2006.

Stevens, J. Harold. "The Influence of New England in Michigan." *MPHC* 19 (1935): 321–53.

Stilwell, Lewis D. *Migration from Vermont.* Montpelier: Vermont Historical Society, 1937.

Stocking, William. "New England Men in Michigan History." *Michigan History Magazine* 5, no. 1–2 (January–April 1921): 123–39.

Streeter, Floyd Benjamin. *Political Parties in Michigan 1837–1860.* Lansing: Michigan Historical Commission, 1918.

Sweet, William Warren. *Religion on the American Frontier, 1783–1850.* Vol. 3, *The Congregationalists.* New York: Cooper Square Publishers, Inc., 1964.

Taber, Morris C. "New England Influence in South Central Michigan." *Michigan History* 45, no. 4 (December 1961): 305–36.

Temin, Peter. "The Industrialization of New England: 1830–1880." In *Engines of Enterprise: The Economic History of New England,* edited by Peter Temin, 109–52. Cambridge, Mass.: Harvard University Press, 1999.

Turner, Frederick Jackson. "Greater New England in the Middle of the Nineteenth Century." *American Antiquarian Society* 29 (October 15, 1919): 222–41.

Ullrich, Pauline Joan. "The Impact of New England Influences Upon the Formative Stages of the Non-Political Institutional Developments in Michigan During the Late Territorial Period." Master's thesis, Wayne State University Press, 1942.

Van Buren, A. D. P. "Pioneer Annals: Containing the History of the Early Settlement of Battle Creek City and Township, with Vivid Sketches of Pioneer Life and Pen Portraits of the Early Settlers." *MPHC* 5 (1884): 237–59.

———. "What the Pioneers Ate and How They Fared—Michigan Food and Cookery in the Early Days." *MPHC* 5 (1884): 293–96.

———. "'Raisings' and 'Bees' Among the Early Settlers." *MPHC* 5 (1884): 296–300.

———. "The Fever and Ague.—'Michigan Rash.'—Mosquitoes—The Old Pioneers' Foes." *MPHC* 5 (1884): 300–304.

———. "The Frolics of Forty-five Years Ago." *MPHC* 5 (1884): 304–309.

Van Nord, Roger. *King of Beaver Island: The Life and Assassination of James Jesse Strang.* Champaign: University of Illinois Press, 1988.

Vinyard, JoEllen McNergney. *For Faith and Fortune: The Education of Catholic Immigrants in Detroit, 1805–1925*. Urbana: University of Illinois Press, 1998.

Wallace, Dewey D. Jr. "Charles Oliver Brown at Dubuque: A Study in the Ideals of Midwestern Congregationalist in the Late Nineteenth Century." *Church History* 53, no. 1 (March 1984): 46–60.

Watkins, Marilyn P. "Civilizers of the West: Clergy and Laity in Michigan Frontier Churches, 1820–1840." In *Michigan: Explorations in its Social History*, edited by Francis X. Blouin Jr. and Maris A. Vinovskis, 161–90. Ann Arbor: Historical Society of Michigan, 1987.

Weber, Max. *The Protestant Ethic and the Spirit of Capitalism*. New York: Charles Scribner's Sons, 1958.

White, George H. "Yankee Lewis' Famous Hostelry in the Wilderness." *MPHC* 26 (1894–95): 302–7.

Widder, Keith R. *Battle for the Soul: Métis Children Encounter Evangelical Protestants at Mackinaw Mission, 1823–1837*. East Lansing: Michigan State University Press, 1999.

Williams, Wolcott B. "New England Influence in Michigan." *MPHC* 17 (1910): 311–19.

Wolcott, Imogene. *The New England Yankee Cookbook*. New York: Coward-McCann, Inc., 1939.

Woodford, Frank B. *Father Abraham's Children: Michigan Episodes in Civil War*. Detroit, Mich.: Wayne State University Press, 1999.

Index